BUILDING
BRIDGES

Wilmer Martin

Building Bridges

President, TourMagination
www.tourmagination.com

Library of Congress Number: 2009902531
ISBN: 978-1-60126-151-9

Scripture references are from the
New Revised Standard Version Bible.

Masthof Press
219 Mill Road
Morgantown, PA 19543-9516
www.masthof.com

DEDICATION

To my wife Janet Ranck Martin, my daughter Janelle, my son Alan, daughter-in-law Christiane, and grandchildren, Matthew and Miriam. My family has blessed me with their love, support and encouragement.

ACKNOWLEDGEMENTS

Thanks to Jan and Barbara Gleysteen and Arnold and Rhoda Cressman, founders of TourMagination, who in 1973 took me as a young pastor on a TourMagination tour when the company was three years old. They invited me to work with them in developing and promoting TourMagination in southwestern Ontario, moving me into tour leadership and allowing me to partner with TourMagination over the last thirty-seven years.

Thanks to Ferne Burkhardt who read and edited the manuscript, encouraged me to find a publisher, underscored that this book could be an inspiration and a resource for the Mennonite World Conference constituency and other Christian and faith groups.

Thanks to Audrey Voth Petkau who felt that producing this book was an inspired idea and would be an inspiration to TourMagination clients. Audrey encouraged me to finish the devotionals and distribute the book to TourMagination clients and also make it available to the broader Mennonite constituency and Christian community.

Thanks to Alana Krause and Brenda Jantzi who typed the first draft and my daughter Janelle Martin for her editing skills.

Thanks to Tyler Petkau who designed the cover. I took the photo of the Bridge of the Americas (Panama Canal).

And thanks, too, to my wife Janet who stood by me, encouraging me to think and write, and for her endless hours of reading the manuscript. Thank you for your love and support and counsel and the skill you bring in editing.

My life has been shaped by those who have called me to serve. In my childhood, I read missionary stories in the *Words of Cheer* and later in the *Youth Christian Companion*. I now realize that I felt called by God to serve, realizing that some day God may call me to be a minister or a missionary. I am grateful for the support of the community that surrounded me including my parents, Omar and Anna Mae Martin; the Chambersburg Mennonite Church, Chambersburg, Pennsylvania; the Tavistock Mennonite Church, Tavistock, Ontario; and the Erb Street Mennonite Church, Waterloo, Ontario. I am blessed by the opportunities I have had in serving with Habitat for Humanity across Canada and in Jamaica, and now by those I meet throughout the world on TourMagination tours and the people with whom we interact.

Contents

FOREWORD

In the church services of our Pennsylvania farm childhood, we loved it when missionaries brought us lesson-teaching curios from "The Field." It was just as welcome to hear a visiting minister say, "Pardon me if I give a personal illustration." Believe me, we had no trouble forgiving what for us was probably the most enjoyable part of the discourse. Emotion! Color! And—perhaps very modestly—a touch of humor! While we quickly forgot the outline (if there was one), some of the narrative vignettes could be remembered life-long.

Historian John Sharp, who has led historical tours for Wilmer and Janet Martin's TourMagination firm, recalls telling a story about a Mennonite preacher who sneezed in mid-sermon, losing a plate of false teeth in the process before catching it in mid-air and returning it into place. The chagrined speaker then complained that though he had been presenting a most valuable theme, "All you are going to remember is my teeth!"

After his talk, narrator Sharp was encouraged to hear an old man confirm, "That's right. I was there when that happened." But what the old fellow added was more significant. He had a special reason, he said, to remember the humorous happening: "That was the night when I gave my heart to the Lord."

What we learn from a story depends on what we bring to hearing it.

A vignette is "a short, impressionistic scene that focuses on one moment or gives a particular insight into a character, idea, or setting."

The harvest of vignettes that gives Wilmer Martin's memoir its texture is non-linear. Evoking a Franklin County, Pennsylvania, dairy farm childhood, it may leap to New Zealand or Calcutta, Antarctica, or Siberia, then double back on itself to make a spiritual point. The logic is that of bringing together what seem to be disparate scenarios, but have a surprising spiritual commonality. The sound of a Pennsylvania farm bell is heard by the farm's grown-up son as it calls people to worship in Tanzania. The values of the congregation ordaining a boy to be preacher will take the adult shape of working with Jimmy Carter in Canada on a house for Habitat for Humanity. A traditional Mennonite sense that true spirituality is also specific will show up—in "MCC" or "MEDA"—as a sharing of practical help as well as verbal doctrine.

Reading Wilmer Martin's memories will bring us to muse: How does one take home-grown values international? How do the boy and girl remain who they are as they become mother and father, then grandparents? How does the freshness, the naïveté of an eighteen-year-old minister segue into the accrual of mature wisdom? What kind of light does travel in seventy countries on seven continents throw back on one's place of birth and upbringing, and vice versa? How is it that while the accumulation of experience seems to coarsen some persons, it refines others? How can some persons regard the narrow parameters of childhood with energizing affection, while others complain lifelong?

While accumulating most of two years myself on buses full of TourMagination clients in Europe, I have savored the narrative leaps of Wilmer's musings, often in the form of devotionals as presented in this book. I have observed them sparking current that then flows between life-stories from our fellow pilgrims. Some are long and detailed; others short and sweet. All are revealing. There is really no story of faith, no vignette, whether told on the bleak island of Patmos or among seven thousand singing assemblees at a World Conference in Zimbabwe that will not have meaning for a listener ready to hear. To paraphrase the cadences of Wilmer Martin's devout youth, "Those who have eyes, let them read."

John L. Ruth
Harleysville, Pennsylvania

PREFACE

This book was written because of the encouragement of many people. Margaret Loewen Reimer, for many years associate editor of the national *Mennonite Reporter* which later became the *Canadian Mennonite*, encouraged me to write down my stories more than twenty years ago when I was chair of the Mennonite Publishing Service board which published the papers. Over the years, I have led many devotionals on TourMagination trips. My goal was always to collect stories that I heard of the Christian Church at work around the world. For the devotionals, I would use a scripture and try to tie it in with what we were experiencing that day as well as connecting it with another part of the Christian Church at work in the world. Tour members affirmed me for the devotionals and said they encouraged them in their Christian lives. Many of them suggested that I publish these stories in a book.

TourMagination tours are planned to fulfill our mission statement, "Building bridges among Mennonites, other Christians and faiths around the world through custom-designed travel." During my decade of working with Habitat for Humanity as president and CEO for Canada and traveling to other countries with Habitat for Humanity International and my work with TourMagination, I have had the opportunity to experience the Christian Church at work in more than seventy countries. I continue to be amazed at the opportunities I have had to interact with Christians and people of other faiths around the world. God is at work, often in surprising ways. I recall in Uzbekistan being moved by the deep faith in God of our Muslim tour guide. It was the first time I had worked for a period of time with a faith Muslim. Christianity and Islam are both missionary religions; however, we chose to interact together and learn from each other's traditions.

I received my seminary degree from Waterloo Lutheran Seminary during my years as pastor at Erb Street Mennonite Church in Waterloo. I took courses, one or two per term, over a seven-year period, but I have always received more energy from functional theology than systematic theology.

Giving pastoral care and walking with people as their pastor when they experienced milestones and challenges in life's journey has always been a joy for me. I enjoyed being a pastor and also my years working for Habitat for Humanity as I walked alongside homeowners and volunteers and celebrated house dedications when another family was freed from living in poverty. This collection of stories interspersed with scriptures is a reminder that God is at work in all continents of the world, wherever his children call upon his name.

I recall a conversation I had with Howard Charles, a professor at Goshen Biblical Seminary where I took a pastoral education course. I said to Dr. Charles, "I wonder when I preach if anyone is listening." He listened to my concern, then said, "Wilmer, for every sermon you preach, there will be someone in the audience for whom God's spirit will use that sermon to encourage them in their walk with God. Keep preaching the word, for as you preach the word you encourage people in their daily living."

As you read this book, perhaps you will remember an incident when you may have been with me on tour. There are other stories that could have been told that reveal God at work through his people. I encourage you, as you have opportunity, to share stories with your faith community, for in doing so we encourage each other in our walk with God.

Wilmer Martin
Waterloo, Ontario

SECTION

STRUGGLES
AND
CHALLENGES

The Art of Being a Pilgrim

O n one of the first days of a tour as part of orienta-
tion, I remind tour members that our bodies travel
easier than our minds. We thrust our bodies across
time zones and our bodies have no choice but to be where we
take them. Our passports remind us of the date and place of
entry into a new country; however, our minds may still be focused on issues related to family, work and home.

TourMagination's mission statement reminds travelers of
the focus of our tours: "Building bridges among Mennonites and
other Christians and faiths around the world." We plan tours
to encourage new discoveries, to create opportunities for new
insights to emerge and we speak of our tours as pilgrimages. The
purpose of a pilgrimage is to make life more meaningful.

When people register for a tour, they are really thinking
of a vacation. They want to see the sights, enjoy great food and
a good place to sleep at the end of the day with all the comforts
of home. And yet, they want their minds to gain new insights,
to learn by seeing, experiencing and listening to new interpretations.

In his writings, known as Analects, Confucius cites practices of wise rulers, five of which are excellent for travelers on a pilgrimage:

1. Practice the arts of attention and listening.
2. Practice renewing yourself every day.
3. Practice meandering toward the center of every place.
4. Practice the ritual of reading sacred texts.
5. Practice gratitude and praise singing.

(From *The Art of Pilgrimage* by Phil Cousineau, page 126.)

Being a pilgrim requires being present in mind where your body is located, of having a spirit of inquiry. One time when my wife Janet and I were leading a tour group through beautiful Wales, we told the group that one of TourMagination's traditions was to give opportunity for fellow travelers who wished to do so to tell part of their life stories. Such sharing allows deeper fellowship, for it reveals common themes. We began by sharing parts of our stories.

Later that evening one of the tour members slipped a piece of paper into my hand and said, "You can read this later." The note brought tears to our eyes. The writer said she appreciated our openness and vulnerability. "I found myself weeping as I heard your stories," she said. "I realized how much I needed this vacation, how much I needed this time away. I became aware of how much I miss my late father. Perhaps I am still grieving his loss. You are so pastoral in the way in which you lead a tour. Thank you for planning and leading this tour and for building bridges of peace and hope through travel."

Being a pilgrim means we are open to learn from our guides who interpret as we travel. We listen not only with our ears, but with our total being. When we visited Dove Cottage in Grasmere, England, our guide told us about the life and history of William Wordsworth. She talked about the relationship he had with Dorothy, his sister, who always lived with William even after he was married. He would dictate poems for Dorothy or his wife Mary to write down on paper. There were times when Dorothy would write something herself and read it to William. Our guide said, that Dorothy was an inspiration to him.

We heard Wordsworth's poem "Daffodils" read to us and later as I walked along the lake I felt the presence of the wind and I could "see" daffodils swaying in the grass. I imagined William Wordsworth, centuries before, thinking as he walked, perhaps on the same path.

In our modern-day living, one of our challenges is the need to compare everything with home. The challenge for a pilgrim is to learn not to compare everything, but to allow one's mind to be present where the body is so that God's spirit can reveal new insights that will bring deeper meaning into one's life.

A good exercise for each of us is to put into a few words our primary aim in life, the motivating factor that goes with us when we get out of bed each morning. Many years ago in a business course, I was one of six executives from across the US and Canada who were connected in a phone conference with an instructor once a month for a year. At one point, we were instructed to write our primary aim and to read it at our next session. I struggled with what to share. I knew that the primary aim I had chosen for my life was from the scriptures: "Love the Lord your God with all your heart, soul and mind and love your neighbor as you love yourself."

I shared Jesus' words with the group when it was my turn to speak. I couldn't see their faces; I could only hear their responses. Our instructor, who was in California, said, "That is a very lofty primary aim." I responded, "It is hard to put into practice, but it is my primary aim."

A continual challenge for a pilgrim is allowing your mind to be where your body is. Driving in the Scottish highlands in a rental car through showers left my spouse and me disappointed since the highlands, covered with heather, were not as beautiful in the rain as we had envisioned. All of a sudden, the sun broke through. Spread across the Scottish highlands was the most spectacular, completely double rainbow we had ever seen. I looked at Janet and said, "Do you know what the rainbow means?"

In our life's pilgrimage, the scriptures remind us that under the rainbow, God will never again forsake his children and destroy the world with a flood. He will ever be with his children as they reach out to him. I was grateful for the conversation, for being present to experience the wonder of being under the rainbow with the person I love.

When we have a discussion about being present, I ask tour members to turn off their cell phones and Blackberries so as not to be interrupted by modern technology and truly be pilgrims. I invite them to trust business or family concerns into God's care. For that day, I suggest that they just experience the wonders, listen to the interpretations of the local guides and use all their senses of sight, sound, smell, touch and taste to take in the magnificence of God's creation.

After a journey in Tajikistan, as our tour group was preparing to leave, the local mayor, a faith Muslim, came to say goodbye to us, a group of Christians who had been guests in his community for three days. He said, "I want to say goodbye to you in the way we Muslims do." He raised his hands with his palms together and then spread them over us and said, "In the name of God." He blessed us as pilgrims and asked us to take his greetings back to our people and to tell them what a blessing we had been as we visited his community. This is being a pilgrim.

CHALLENGED BY OVERWHELMING SITUATIONS

A t the University of the West Indies in Kingston, Jamaica, our group of young people was informed that Jamaica, considering its population, statistically is the killing capital of the world. That statement overwhelmed our group. The political history, which has led to violence, has created these "killings" and the ghettos amidst the beautiful country of Jamaica. But our group didn't experience any violence, only the warmth of the people.

In Calcutta, India, a city of twenty-two million people, forty percent of the population lives in tremendous poverty. The air is constantly heavy with smog. Many cook, bath and sleep on the streets. It was a challenge not to be overwhelmed with the poverty in India.

My spirit was lifted in visiting the House of Destitute and Dying in Calcutta. It is where Mother Teresa's program began more than fifty years ago. Men and women are brought into this home when they are dying on the streets. A former German banker welcomed us and before we left, he asked us to sing a song for the men in the crowded room. As we sang, he sat and held one of the men who was dying. He had found his place and purpose in life.

The Apostle Paul in his letter to the young church at Philippi gave some guidance which can assist us who are challenged and overwhelmed by situations in which we find ourselves. He suggests in Philippians 4 that we rejoice in God's presence. This means recognizing that God is near and hears our requests as we come to him in prayer.

If the late Mother Teresa, who had made a vow of poverty, was given more than enough food for the day, she shared the food with those in need around her and kept only enough for herself for that day. She said, "God will provide for tomorrow."

There are times when we wonder if we make a difference. After being at the University of West Indies, our group drove through Majesty Gardens, one of the ghettos in Kingston where Habitat for Humanity Jamaica has built more than forty homes. There is still tremendous poverty and yet in the midst of this need, we saw signs of hope. A home provides security and a place where people can be renewed to face a new day. I felt joy to see how the community has changed since the first forty homes were built there more than ten years ago.

As we drove back across the mountains, the young people began to sing songs they had sung during their high school years. The grade twelve students, in their last month prior to graduation, were required to have this intercultural experience. Many of them felt overwhelmed by what they had experienced—poverty and wealth, crime and death which they had heard about earlier in the day and couldn't understand. Our coach driver and I looked at each other. When we arrived at the villa and they were all off the coach, he put his hand across his heart and said, "We had an amazing day experiencing beautiful Jamaica as we went across the mountains, going from the north coast to the south coast. We saw the change in Majesty Gardens and we heard these young people singing from their hearts their love for humanity and for God."

When you find your purpose in life, the miraculous may occur. Opportunities can emerge in a situation that seems hopeless. God can help us use these opportunities to bring about change and hope.

SUFFERING

"If one member suffers, all suffer together with it; if one member is honored, all rejoice together with it" (I Corinthians 12:26).

Suffering is central throughout our history as members of the Anabaptist believers church. Suffering is defined as a state of mind when one is in anguish or pain or bearing loss. For the Anabaptists in the early 1500s, suffering occurred because they chose not to follow the mandate of the state and the church but to follow their conscience and faith. Because of this choice, the *Martyrs Mirror* is filled with stories of people who suffered exile from home and country, loss of property and, for many, even their lives.

Menno Simons, our earliest leader from the Netherlands, wrote, "True evangelical faith cannot lie dormant. It clothes the naked, it feeds the hungry, it comforts the sorrowful, it shelters the destitute, it serves those that harm it, it binds up that which is wounded, it has become all things to all people."

On a TourMagination trip in Zimbabwe, an African Brethren in Christ pastor asked me, "As a Mennonite minister in Canada, how many orphans do you have in your congregation?" When I answered him that we do not have any orphans, he seemed surprised. He has thirty-eight orphans in his congregation. Then he asked how many individuals in my parish have died of AIDS. Again I quietly said, "We don't have any people who have died of AIDS and I'm not aware of anybody in our congregation who suffers from the disease." He looked somewhat stunned and asked, "Why is it that God has placed this burden of suffering on our congregation? Why do we suffer from AIDS when you, brothers and sisters in North America, are not suffering in this way?"

On a tour in Siberia, our group was visiting the village of Neustadt. We were privileged to have a conversation with Brother Wall, an eighty-nine-year-old minister who had spent more than eighteen years of his life in a prison in northern Siberia. At one time there were no men, young or old, left in the village of Neustadt. It was illegal to attend church but in the midst of all this suffering, the women never ceased to be the church. They continued to read their Bibles privately and to encourage each other in their homes.

Brother Wall spent more than eighteen years in prison camps. He told how, at thirty or forty degrees below zero, men with hardly any food in their stomachs were sent out to cut lumber in the forest. Trees were frozen solid and saws bounced against the frozen wood. One day, as an eighteen-year-old boy, he fell in the snow, too weak to stand up. He would have frozen to death except that his colleagues knew that if they returned to camp with one prisoner missing, all the rest of the prisoners would suffer. So they carried him back to camp and, miraculously, he was sent back to his home. His mother nursed him back to health by spooning warm soup into him and praying. He said, "If this hadn't happened in the midst of all the suffering, I would have died a sinner. Because of my mother's prayer and nourishment I found salvation."

Brother Wall was arrested and sent to prison camps at different times, but after the fall of the iron curtain in 1991, a meetinghouse was built in Neustadt and today the villagers have freedom of worship.

One member of our group asked Brother Wall, "When Stalin died, did the Mennonites rejoice or did they do as the Soviets did, taking saliva from their mouths and putting it into their eyes to make it look like they were crying even though they were rejoicing inside?" The room was silent; I heard the clock ticking on the wall. Then Brother Wall said quietly, "No, we did not rejoice; we prayed, for the Bible tells us to pray for those placed in authority over us." He said that they continued to pray in the midst of all the suffering. "We are so grateful that the women never stopped being the church and today our meetinghouse is full."

The words of I Corinthians 12:26 remind us that when one member suffers, we all suffer together. Menno Simons said that true evangelical faith cannot lie dormant for it provides food for those who are hungry and help to those who are suffering. Today as the world is connected by mass media, the internet and instant pictures, we are often overwhelmed as how to respond to those who are suffering and frustrated when help offered or given is not accepted or does not reach the recipient.

When you recognize you have been blessed, you understand there is a responsibility that comes with that blessing. I remind myself and my fellow travelers on tour that when we leave a country and return to our homes, we have a responsibility to share from the knowledge that we have gained. We pray that we may go home a little kinder, a little more loving.

"Jesus, help us live in peace, from our blindness set us free. Fill us with your healing love. Help us live in unity" (Gerald Derstine, 1971).

SURVIVAL

On a tour in Norway, we traveled on a beautiful fjord with spectacular mountain ranges, sometimes rising fifteen hundred meters from the water. The giant cliffs were covered with trees that seemed to grow straight up to heaven. Some of the high peaks were snowcapped. Before we could absorb one scene, the next one would appear and be just as dramatic, if not more so. Occasionally we would see a small picturesque farm, isolated from everything, with no road apparent. We wondered how they survived.

Our guide informed us that once or twice a week a water taxi brought supplies and took the farmer and his family to an appointment if they needed to leave the farm. He informed us that, for many of the farmers, survival depended on the water taxi, but they are not lonely. Today this isolated Norwegian community is connected to the rest of the world by satellite.

In I Corinthians 12, the young church at Corinth was reminded of the gifts that each person brings to the community. Chapter 13 reminded them that the skills and gifts they bring to the community must be expressed through love, because love is patient and kind, it is not envious or boastful, it does not rejoice in wrongdoing, but rejoices in the truth (verses 4-6).

Eli Landis from Bucks County, Pennsylvania was a farmer and a hunter. He liked hunting for moose in Canada. On one of his hunting trips in the middle 1960s, Eli bought several farms for himself and his sons in the community of Hunta in the Cochrane area of northern Ontario. They talked a neighbor into moving to Canada with them. After the four families settled in northern Ontario, Eli said, "We must meet for worship." He asked Eastern Mennonite Missions to assist them in formalizing a church community. Eli, the first appointed leader, was named the superintendent. Bishop Raymond Charles of the Mission Board, a cousin of my father, knew I was a minister in Tavistock, Ontario. He asked me to visit these Pennsylvania Mennonites and encourage them to relate to the Mennonite community in Ontario. Although Hunta was 500 miles away from the nearest Mennonite congregation, it was much closer than churches in Pennsylvania.

During the 1970s, 80s and 90s, it was my privilege to visit this community of faith on many occasions. They had challenges related to Americans settling in Canada where traditions and practices, particularly in the Ontario conference, were different. They also faced isolation and problems with tourists coming into the community for hunting. Yet, in the midst of all the challenges, they experienced God's sustaining presence.

The first time I met one person who lived alone in the community, I thought she was a man. She ran a beef operation and her farms were 25 miles apart. On one visit to Hunta, church people informed me that we needed to help Dorothy bale straw on her farm on the other side of Cochrane. So on Saturday afternoon, a group of us went to help her. Then on Sunday, the church held a community worship service and picnic at one of the farms followed by games and visiting. Dorothy sat there watching adults and children play baseball. She asked me why we came to help her bring in her straw the previous day. She said, "We in the north have been a community, but this action brings community and support to a different and higher level." A year or two later, men from the congregation stopped by to check on Dorothy. They discovered she was very ill so the community helped look after her cattle for more than a month until her health was restored.

Today Hunta Mennonite Church is more than thirty-five years old. It is an established community church begun by the vision of the late Eli Landis and is a member of Mennonite Church Eastern Canada. It is a testimony to a group of believers who reached out, united by scripture and the desire to be a community of faith under the Mennonite Church umbrella. A testament to this congregation could be summed up in the words of Lauchlan M. Watt in 1907:

> *"I bind my heart this tide to the Galilean's side,*
> *to the wounds of Calvary,*
> *to the Christ who died for me.*
>
> *I bind my soul this day to the neighbor far away,*
> *and the stranger near at hand,*
> *in this town, and in this land.*
>
> *I bind my heart in thrall to the God, the Lord of all,*
> *to the God, the poor one's friend,*
> *and the Christ whom he did send.*
>
> *I bind myself to peace, to make strife and envy cease.*
> *God, knit thou sure the cord*
> *of my thralldom to my Lord! Amen "*

(From *Hymnal: A Worship Book,* Brethren Press, Elgin, Illinois; Faith and Life Press, Newton, Kansas; Mennonite Publishing House, Scottdale, Pennsylvania, 1992*)*

KNOWING
WHO WE ARE

O n one of our tours, a tour member found a necklace lying on the gangplank while embarking the
cruise ship. She did the right thing. She turned in
the necklace to our tour leader who in turn took it to the lost
and found desk on the cruise ship. I was pleased that the tour
member and our tour leader acted with integrity and turned in
the necklace to be claimed by the rightful owner.

This incident caused considerable conversation among
the group as they met the next day for conversation and devo-
tions. Some wondered why the article was turned in. Others
thought that the necklace should be retrieved from the lost and
found desk and brought back to the person who found it. The
conversation helped our group focus on the community.

During my years serving as a pastor I used Matthew 5,
6 and 7, Jesus' Sermon on the Mount, for many of my sermons
and for conversations with our youth. Jesus said, "You are the
light of the world. A city built on a hill cannot be hid.... Let your
light shine before others, so that they may see your good works
and give glory to your Father in heaven" (Matthew 5:14).

TourMagination has worked with Hani, president and CEO of Near East Travel, for more than twenty-five years. He is a Christian-Palestinian who, with his brother, operates a business that his father began in Jerusalem. Some time ago I told Hani that he is too fond of the Mennonites and gives us more credit than we deserve. Then he told me a story.

Hani said, "Wilmer, you do not know why I am so fond of Mennonites. More than twenty years ago I had a deep concern for the Palestinians. They had no credit union and no place to do their banking in the West Bank.

"In a conversation with a Mennonite businessman, I expressed my concern: If only we had some capital! With $5,000 we could start a credit union so that the people in the West Bank would have a place to do their banking. I had no capital; I only had a vision. I do not remember the man's name, but he loaned me $5,000 and a group of us formed a credit union. The loan has long been paid back with interest. Today that little credit union is known as the PBC, the Palestine Banking Corporation, with its head office in Ramallah and offices in Jerusalem and other West Bank cities. How can I not be fond of you Mennonites? You put your words into action and you don't do it for personal glory."

When people focus on the community rather than self, they are known by their deeds and their fruits follow them. Pastor James Wuye and Imam Mohammed Ashafa of Nigeria were the co-recipients of the Tannenbaum Peace Award in 2000. I heard them speak at Conrad Grebel University College. These two men had been enemies, determined to kill each other. It is a miracle of God's grace that today they are working together to build peace because the Imam lost two of his sons to Pastor James' militia men and Pastor James lost his arm to the Imam's militia men. They said, "Be aware how your actions locally affect [people] globally." Pastor James said, "My past will always haunt me; however, we can always make the world more peaceable by working towards peace. Let us understand our differences, so we can build understanding."

COMMITMENT

On a tour to China we visited Amity Foundation, an organization similar to Mennonite Central Committee. We were impressed with the ministry of Amity all across China. The astonishing and quite unpredictable explosion of the number of Christans in recent years is clearly connected to a widespread sense of God at work. We had a vivid sense of what a watershed moment this was for the whole country.

Ted, our local guide in Wuxi, told us that eighty percent of the people of China have no belief. They believed in communism, but communism failed them. Today, fewer than one percent of Chinese people are Christian, yet there are more than eighteen million Christians in the country. A small, but powerful seed has been sown. God is doing great things.

Kathy, our guide in China, was glad to know that we were a Christian group. Her husband was a Christian and she was curious about Christianity. It was wonderful working with Kathy. Janet and I bought her an English/Chinese Bible and had the opportunity to discuss spiritual issues with her. At the end of the tour, she said to Janet and me, "I hope I can be good enough to be a Christian." We encouraged her to continue to read God's word and stay in touch with us by email so that we could walk with her in her spiritual journey.

Another guide in China told us the following story: "A turtle and a rabbit had a race to see who was the fastest and the smartest animal. The rabbit said, "Of course, I am the fastest," but the turtle agreed to a race. They agreed on the destination. The rabbit and the turtle started off at the same time and the rabbit ran fast. He knew that the turtle was far behind him, so he decided to lie down and have a snooze. The turtle got to the destination first. The rabbit said, "It's not fair. You were so slow, and I stopped and slept." So they agreed to have another race. This time the turtle chose the destination. Again they took off, the rabbit running fast, the turtle coming more slowly. The rabbit got to a river that he had to cross. When the turtle arrived, the rabbit said, "It's not fair, I can't swim across like you can." The turtle said to the rabbit, "Why don't you crawl on my back and sit on my shoulders, and I will swim across. Then we can both reach the destination and we will both be winners." The rabbit accepted the offer. Commitment requires cooperation and partnership.

Anglican Archbishop Williams, the Archbishop of Canterbury wrote: "On our visit in China we have seen how the church vigorously pursued the vision of Christ. In some regions of China, the percentage of the population of China attending church on Sunday is at least as large, and in some cases larger, than in most Western European countries. We have seen projects on children's welfare, rural health care, advocacy for migrants and many other concerns which a church has taken up, and we applaud the willingness of the church to provide support. If China is to develop a kind of civil society that will guarantee both stability and harmony; the church is a vital partner." He went on: "We saw a striking example of the state's recognition of this with a statement of a very senior government figure about the potential significance of the church's Sunday school program. The government official said, 'The Christian church school is backing up the growth of a mature and stable public morality.'"

One of the ministries our tour group visited in Sydney, Australia was operated by Ross and Di, Christian workers in an area of Sydney called Glebe. They work with people on social assistance, some of whom have mental and sexual dysfunctions and other difficulties, persons who are forgotten.

They introduced us to a new member of their team, a cute puppy. Our group named him Menno. They explained why they bought the dog. Di said, "When you walk in the street with a young baby in a stroller, people stop and talk with you. We found that Menno causes people to stop and talk with us. It gives us an opportunity to learn to know them, to share God's love, to invite them to Bible study and to walk with them. We find that we are learning so much from the community in Glebe." Ross and Di are examples of people who deny themselves to serve others. We were impressed with their commitment and their desire to share God's love.

One of the wonderful sights our tour group enjoyed in Australia was visiting Ayers Rock or as the Aborigines call it, Uluru. Mel, our driver-guide, enjoys interpreting the history and the culture of Ayers Rock. For the Aborigines, it is a sacred place. Mel shared with us many of the teachings that the Aborigines have accepted over the centuries and how they see and feel God's spirit speaking to them. Mel more than once said, "Try to think outside the squares, so that you can learn from the Aborigines."

Each morning our group sang a hymn, we read scripture and had prayer. I or other tour members commented on a theme related to the scripture or to what was happening. Mel said to me, "Your people are my people; God willing we will see each other again."

In 1960, the Mennonite Church in Pennsylvania was interested in beginning mission work in Guatemala. Today, there is a thriving Mennonite church in Guatemala as a result of the initiative of Mennonites of Franklin County, Pennsylvania. Our bishop spoke against beginning this mission work. Why would he do such a thing? For him, being a follower of Jesus Christ meant certain patterns, a particular standard of dress and code of thinking. He was honest in saying that mission work brings in new people and new interpretation and he was afraid that the new seed would bring with it counterfeit rather than genuine faith.

I am glad Bishop Martin did not veto the mission program. He was tolerant and allowed it to go ahead even though he had questions and no personal commitment to bringing Christ's message to the people of Guatemala. No doubt he knew that this was a new wind of God's Spirit and that the church would have to discern what is genuine and what is counterfeit as they followed Jesus Christ.

Today the Christian church is spreading all over the world due to the commitment of people like our friends Don and Eunice who have been missionaries with Wycliffe Bible Translators for more than thirty years. They rely on God to provide for their financial needs through the gifts of interested individuals and churches. We have been moved by their faith and commitment to bring the Bible into the language of the people.

Vision—Like a Gentle Breeze

I Kings 19:11 and 12 describe Elijah as standing on a mountain. First a great and mighty wind tore into the mountain and broke the rocks into pieces. The story boldly asserts that the Lord is not in the wind. Then the earth quaked, but the Lord was not in the earthquake. Next came a fire, but the Lord was not in the fire. Finally, there was a still small voice. The contrast is powerful: wind, earthquake, fire! All noisy, destructive forces, the opposite of peace. Then, all of a sudden, a still, small voice.

Dr. Dan Miller shared a devotional at a MEDA (Mennonite Economic Development Associates) convention in Columbus, Ohio. He asked, "What does it mean to speak as a gentle whisper, both personally and corporately? God has called us to be his disciples, to make him known to others, to love our neighbors as ourselves. Many Christians prefer the gentle whisper approach."

Why is it that people get excited and admire the aggressive behavior, many times bordering on violence, exhibited on Hockey Night in Canada? The world in which we live is big on the wind, the earthquake, the fire approach, not the gentle whisper or the quiet in the land.

Each generation struggles to identify its vision and focus as a Christian church. Luke 4 records Jesus' vision of change: "He has sent me to bring good news to the oppressed, to bind up the brokenhearted, to proclaim liberty and relief in the year of the Lord's favor." Jesus' message, clearly his vision for the future, comes like an earthquake.

I enjoy reading the letters to the editor in the church papers. They are conversations about what it means to be the church. One reader wrote, "Mennonite Church USA can talk all it wants about being missional, but if we can't even figure out why people leave, what's the point of all that fine talk?" She wants *The Mennonite* to print occasional stories like 'Why I'm not a Mennonite anymore,' or 'Why I am still a Mennonite, but its touch and go sometimes' or 'Why I'd love to be a Mennonite, if only...' The author of this letter is asking through conversation to discover together how God will deliver and restore his people with glory.

During the 2008 US presidential election campaign, editorials in newspapers in South America and Europe were enthusiastic about Barack Obama even before he became President-Elect. Why were people around the world so excited? Because he listened. He wanted to assist people in their goal of health and prosperity.

Janet and I heard an executive with the Evangelical Church in Ohio speak on an evangelical radio station. He made it clear that he and most of his listeners had voted Republican but he asked people to pray for President-Elect Obama, and he said that Obama is a fine Christian man. "Even though he may have a different opinion on some issues, we need to support him so that God can use him for his honor and his glory," he said. Janet and I looked at each other and said, "Now that's a wonderful Christian attitude. Here is good news!"

Recently, I was having lunch with several people with whom I serve as director on a corporate board. Instead of talking about board business, we were talking about the church. Around the table were Mennonite, Lutheran and United Church of Canada members. Someone asked me about the status of the Mennonite Church today. I stated that I am very hopeful about the Mennonite Church, its leaders, its place in the world and its efforts to follow Jesus Christ. I also stated that in North America we have challenges and that some numbers are going down instead of up, whereas in many countries the church is growing very quickly. People are excited about being Christian and following Jesus Christ in spite of persecution and suffering.

Two directors were from the Lutheran Church. One was excited about his congregation and the other was talking about how his large church has low attendance and little life. I was amazed when the other director turned to him and said, "If your church is dying, it's because of you. Instead of going to church, you watch football and instead of supporting the church and praying for your pastor, you are blaming your church's downfall on your pastor. It's not your pastor's fault, it's your problem."

Life is about choices. We choose whether we want to be part of this wonderful movement that is taking place that gives Christians in many countries so much energy. We have to choose to be citizens of this new kingdom. We have to choose to assist the oppressed, the brokenhearted, those who are captive, and those who need to be released.

Ernst Eitzen from Filadelfia, Paraguay, told me a story when we were together. A 74-year-old German widow lives alone on a huge tract of land in the Chaco in Paraguay. She hired a Mennonite and some Indigenous people to build a fence and a road to her ranch. Then she went to Germany. When she came back, after the road and fence were built, she fired the workers and refused to pay them. She said, "I told you to build the road straight in. You built it in and over and up and then in. You didn't build it the way I said." The workers said, "We couldn't build it as you asked. We had to go two kilometers around the swamp." She said, "I don't care. You didn't do it the way I said, so I am not going to pay you."

Sometime later the widow came to Ernst Eitzen. She wanted him to teach her Spanish, so she could communicate with her neighbors. While teaching her Spanish, he learned the story of the road and the fence. He said to her, "If you are going to succeed in Paraguay out there all by yourself in the Chaco, you have to work with the Paraguayans. If you are willing to work with them you will succeed; otherwise, you will fail. Your heart is like stone."

About three months later the woman came back to him. She said, "I want to thank you for what you said. I paid the workers and hired them back. I asked for their forgiveness." Ernst said, "This is our message. If we're going to be part of the new order, we need to have a clear vision and live lives of openness and integrity."

Luke's Gospel tells the story of Mary and Martha. Martha welcomes Jesus into their home, then goes into another room to do something important while Mary sits and listens in Jesus' presence. Like Elijah, Mary was able to hear the gentle whisper of God. Because she was listening, Mary received the blessing. God does not force himself on us. God comes to those who welcome him. When we allow God to walk with us, we find new life in Jesus' teachings.

Lord, make us instruments of your peace.
Where there is hatred, let us sow love;
   where there is injury, pardon;
   where there is doubt, faith;

where there is despair, hope;
where there is sadness, joy.
In the name of Jesus Christ, Amen.

(Adapted from the prayer of St. Francis of Assisi)

THE WORD IS COURAGE

Anabaptist history goes back to 1525. Discerning the scriptures and faith is central to the beginning of this Believers Church movement. The Grossmünster Cathedral was a place of activity in Zurich, Switzerland. People came there to debate issues related to faith with Bible teacher Ulrich Zwingli, a great orator and early Reformer. The Swiss brethren, George Blaurock, Felix Manz and Conrad Grebel, were attracted to Ulrich Zwingli. The Bible came alive to these students under his teaching; however, there were several points important to them that Zwingli seemed to overlook. As they studied the Bible, they concluded that the church and the state should be separate and that the Bible taught the way of peace. Zwingli, however, was appointed to the Grossmünster Cathedral by the state, not the people, and he was the chaplain of the Zurich army.

These young Swiss students also thought that people should be baptized upon confession of faith. Zwingli continued to baptize infants and register them as citizens of Zurich and of the state. Zwingli was very fond of Blaurock, Manz and Grebel, as these young scholars were prize students and good communicators of the Reformation. But Zwingli couldn't keep them in line. On January 21, 1525, as they were meeting in Anna Manz's home, George Blaurock took a pitcher of water from the kitchen table, knelt down and said to Conrad Grebel, "In the name of Christ, give me the true baptism." Approximately 16 others received baptism at that time. We look back to this event as the beginning of the Believers Church, the Anabaptist movement, and to these three Swiss brethren as our founders. Yet history records that all three of them were dead within two years of their baptism.

Felix Manz was drowned for his faith in the Limmat River because he chose to stay true to his faith and not to denounce what he believed. History suggests that his mother and brother stood on the shore encouraging him to remain true to his faith. George Blaurock was beaten out of Zurich, captured in Klausen, Italy and lost his life. Conrad Grebel died of the plague. Today we sing the hymn, "I sing with exaltation," written by Felix Manz, which reveals extreme courage in following Jesus Christ:

I sing with exaltation, all my heart's delight
is God who brings salvation, frees from death's dread might.
I praise thee, Christ of heaven, who ever shall endure,
who takes away my sorrow, keeps me safe and secure.

Christ bids us, none compelling, to his glorious throne.
They only who are willing Christ as Lord to own,
they are assured of heaven, who will right faith pursue,
with hearts made pure through penance, sealed with baptism true.

(From *Hymnal: A Worship Book*, Brethren Press, Elgin, Illinois; Faith and Life Press, Newton, Kansas; Mennonite Publishing House, Scottdale, Pennsylvnia, 1992*)*

Psalm 27 says: "When evildoers assail me, uttering slanders against me, my adversaries and foes, they shall stumble and fall.... For he will hide me in his shelter in the day of trouble; he will conceal me under the cover of his tent; he will set me high upon a rock.... I will sing and make melody to the Lord" (verses 2, 5 and 6b).

Have you observed that you are better able to cope with life's complexities and to have more courage and confidence when you have taken time to feed on God's word? I find that it is in the quiet, calm, early hours of the morning when, symbolically, the waters are still that God speaks to me. My soul is nurtured and I come away from these times of meditation, reflection and communion with Christ refreshed in mind and spirit.

Ed Epp served with Mennonite Central Committee in the Middle East. He shared that the Muslims, whose religious leader is called Imam, believe God (Allah) is great and that there is nothing God cannot do. They believe that Jesus could be God's son, but they have trouble accepting the trinity and believing that God's son would die on the cross.

Both Christianity and Islam are missionary religions. One day Ed stopped in a village and the Imam tried to convert Ed to Islam. Finally Ed said to the Imam, "God is great. Do you agree with that?" "Yes," he replied. "There is nothing that God could not do. Do you believe this?" Ed continued. The Imam said "yes." "So then God could have sent his son Jesus to the world to die on the cross for our sins and to rise again? God could do that, couldn't he?" The Imam threw up his hands and walked away. Ed said, "I left, feeling I had won the debate."

Ed didn't see the Imam for some time after that. About a month later Ed was asked to deliver the one thousand seedlings the Imam had ordered. He got to the village and was unloading the seedlings when the Imam came and asked, "What are you doing?" Ed explained, "I was coming this way. I was told you ordered these seedlings so I'm delivering them for you." The Imam said, "Why would you do that when you hate me?" Ed replied, "I don't hate you." The Imam invited him in for tea and they shared a conversation.

Ed reminded our group that in order to share Christ's love and for successful dialogue there must be four components: 1) we should live together, be neighborly and interact with each other; 2) we should work and do projects together; 3) we should discuss theology and spirituality together; and 4) we should recognize the goodness in each other even though there are points where we disagree.

In 1997 Janet and I were in Calcutta, India, with a group attending the Mennonite World Conference assembly. I very much wanted our group to visit Mother Teresa's program in Calcutta, especially the Motherhouse, the orphanage and the house for the destitute and dying. We made an appointment to meet Mother Teresa and have her speak to our group. I was very excited. I wanted to be able to kiss her hand and tell her what an inspiration she had been to me in my ministry.

We arrived at the Motherhouse and found that Mother Teresa was sick in bed. The Mother Superior met us and talked with us instead. Initially I was disappointed. We were overwhelmed when we discovered how many babies the sisters had collected from the streets of Calcutta that morning.

I learned something that morning in the Motherhouse when I was unable to meet my spiritual mentor. I observed her presence through hand-written messages on the chalkboard, the spirit of God's grace in the Motherhouse and by watching the volunteers working.

"I believe that I shall see the goodness of the Lord in the land of the living. Wait for the Lord; be strong and let your heart take courage" (Psalm 27:13-14).

LIVING STONES

He came into our family as a boy who needed a place to live and a family who cared, a place where he could work, use his skills and make some money to support himself. He was only sixteen. Our farm family met all of those requirements.

I still remember my mother, Anna Mae, who had already mothered four boys, saying that day, "Oh no! You mean I have to be a mother to another boy? I thought my load was getting lighter." My mother's response revealed to me that she saw her role as a mother not as a job to fulfill, but as a ministry. My mother was a spiritual woman. She enjoyed being a pastor's wife and going with my father to visit the sick and shut-ins in their homes or in the hospital. She enjoyed welcoming friends into our home for Bible study and prayer meetings.

My mother died of heart failure within two years of accepting another boy into our home. Her death sent shock-waves through our family. We prayed and worked together in the midst of tragedy and accepted a lot of love and support from our church family. Our lives centered around our farm and were rooted in the scriptures and in our church family. My brothers and I discussed the strong values that our parents passed on to us.

I Peter 2:9 and 10 read: "But you are a chosen race, a royal priesthood, a holy nation. God's own people, in order that you may proclaim the mighty acts of him who called you out of darkness into his marvelous light. Once you were not a people, now you are God's people; once you had not received mercy, but now you have received mercy." And verse 4, "Come to him, a living stone, though rejected by mortals yet chosen and precious in God's sight."

Peter says that Jesus Christ is a living stone. That may not make sense to us. A stone is cold and heavy; living speaks of life. How can Jesus Christ be a living stone? Peter is talking of Jesus Christ as the foundation for the Christian church.

Mario and Egda Snyder are retired missionaries in Argentina. On a tour to South America our group spent two days in Buenos Aires. Mario and Egda were our guests. Mario, a native of Ontario, and Egda, a native of Argentina, shared with us their excitement of the growth of the church in Argentina in 2008.

We asked Mario how he accounts for the fact that the church in Argentina is growing so quickly. He said, "In South America people take more time to be present in the situation. We don't move as quickly as in North America. We take time with one another and feel and appreciate the concerns expressed with genuine care."

Mario sees his role as helping to provide light, to walk with pastors and their families so that they can provide strong leadership to the growing church communities. "A missionary minister never retires; he just changes gears and slows down," he said.

Another tour group visited the dynamic growing church in Peru. In the heart of the city of Cusco on a Thursday afternoon, the Mennonite congregation, geared toward university students, welcomed us with music and singing. Then we went into the country and visited four communities where the church is alive and growing. The group had prepared a meal for us that they would have served at a wedding or festive occasion: roasted guinea pig, baked potatoes and roasted corn on the cob. As members of the family of God, they wanted to welcome North American members of the same family.

Our last stop before returning to Cusco was a site where workers were beginning to pour the footers for the foundation of a new building. The minister explained his vision for a church and school so that they could train the next generation. Our group of thirty-three was so moved that someone suggested we lay hands on the leaders and pray that God might bless, protect and watch over this project. Then we passed the hat so people could make donations to the project.

Two years later on another tour, I was impressed that a building was standing and a wedding was to take place there the next day. The building was not finished, but finished sections were being used for worship. They told us that the day our group left two years ago, they bought materials with the money we donated. They proceed with building only as God provides the resources.

In the Lima region of Peru, there is a church in one of the poor boroughs that has been built with the love and support of TourMagination groups. In 2004, our tour group had a most profound experience. Pastor Tony asked us to visit several of the boroughs where he was working with villagers. Our bus followed Pastor Tony and when we got off the bus, we saw thousands of people living in a community with no running water. Water was brought by a truck and put into a tank.

Pastor Tony unlocked a door and we walked in and stood on a concrete pad with bamboo sides and a bamboo roof. He explained that his vision was to have a church building here with facilities so that children who came to worship could get a bath, have breakfast; learn life skills in a Sunday school program that used the Bible as the foundation, and get a drink and a biscuit for their lunch before they were sent home in the early afternoon.

One of the businessmen in our group said, "Ask Pastor Tony how much money he needs to complete the structure and invite him and his wife to join us for dinner at our hotel. We will present him with a donation." I was grateful for this level of generosity.

That evening as Pastor Tony and his wife joined us for dinner at the hotel, our group presented him with the cash to buy the steel to complete the walls and the roof. Two years later, another group was in the area. We saw that the structure was indeed built and that group gave a donation for windows and washrooms. When we have the love of Christ within us, we want to reach out and help our neighbors.

THE PERSISTENCE OF EVIL

I f God is God, why does he allow the tragedies that we hear about in the media to happen? Jesus' fascinating story in Matthew 13 tells about weeds growing among the wheat. It highlights a social problem called spitefulness. The farmer has carefully prepared the soil and he goes to the seed dealer and buys clean, high-quality seed and sows his field of wheat.

When the task is completed, unknown to him, an enemy comes and deliberately sows weeds among his wheat. The problem, according to the text, is that the damage is irreversible because you can't tell what is wheat and what is weeds. The weed sown was a special kind of plant called darnel. It spoiled the crop not only because it takes nutrients from the soil as it grows among the wheat seedlings but it is a plant that looks like wheat. The difference between the plants doesn't show up until the time of harvest. Then the darnel's head is empty.

This parable shows us that good and evil are not always easy to distinguish but it reminds us to hope in God's victory and to live with courage.

From 1968 to 1978, as pastor of the Tavistock Mennonite Church, I discovered that key leaders in Grace United Church and Trinity Lutheran Church in the community were baptized as Mennonites. In the 1940s and 1950s, many Mennonite young people joined these churches where they had found partners. They felt welcomed and that God was at work in the churches of their spouses. In that era, Mennonite leaders considered these young people to be weeds among their church family and they did not work to gather them into their fold. They allowed them to blow away. These people turned out to be very fine Lutheran or United Church members as they served Christ in these denominations.

This parable of Jesus can serve as a caution for us as we think about evil in our midst. The caution relates to where we put our focus. The parable teaches us to hope in God's victory. We are called to welcome all God's children, recognizing that we won't be a perfect community. We are to be an inclusive family of faith, teach the scriptures and call people to recognize God's presence. As we discern together, we will challenge one another to follow Christ faithfully.

In July 2008, robbers attacked the Bergens from British Columbia who were missionaries in Kenya. The guards at their compound joined the attackers who robbed them, leaving them for dead. However, their lives were spared. The Bergens told their children that they feel called to stay in Kenya and serve in the name of Christ. "God will protect us," they said. "Our work is not yet finished. God has spared us for a purpose."

Eileen Coffman and her late husband John were a missionary couple at the London Mennonite Centre in England. In 1987, when England was fighting Argentina over the Falkland Islands, the Coffmans were part of our TourMagination European Heritage tour. Eileen shared with us that every Sunday morning the Church of England was asked to pray for the soldiers who were fighting in the Falklands. This prayer request was broadcast over radio and television. Eileen wrote a letter to the Archbishop of the Church of England, asking the church to pray for soldiers on both sides of the conflict, including the Argentinean soldiers.

Jesus calls us to view life neither optimistically nor pessimistically, but humbly and faithfully as his followers. The persistence of evil is here, but the reality of God's presence is much stronger.

Prayer: Dear God, we thank you that even though evil is in our midst, it will not triumph. Comfort those who feel overwhelmed by darkness. Help them to remember that you will never leave or forsake your children. Amen.

BE CAREFUL
WHAT YOU PRAY

The year was 1999. I was serving as president and CEO of Habitat for Humanity Canada as well as president of TourMagination. Both companies were doing well. I was working seven days and eighty-plus hours a week and both organizations required more time. My family said that I needed to decide whether to continue my role with Habitat for Humanity. If so, I should sell TourMagination. It was a dilemma I did not know how to solve since I loved both programs and enjoyed growing them and I felt they were both God's work.

In late November as my plane was approaching Vancouver airport, I was in the washroom freshening up, preparing for my appointment after the plane landed. I leaned my forehead against the mirror, saying, "God, I'm tired. I don't know how to solve this problem. Habitat for Humanity Canada is your ministry and I'm your servant. TourMagination is your ministry and I'm your servant. I don't know how to continue to guide both programs. I place them both into your care."

I was thrust into leadership at age 18 when I was chosen by lot and ordained at the Chambersburg Mennonite Church in Pennsylvania. This meant that I was called to serve as one of its ministers. A minister was expected to make his own living as he served his congregation. I had just finished high school; I already owned several cows and planned to be part of the family business.

In those early years as a minister and farmer, I clung to two verses written by Paul to young Timothy. "Don't allow anyone to make fun of you because of your youth and leadership" (I Timothy 4:12). And second, "I can do all things through Christ who strengthens me" (Philippians 4:13). I also remember praying, "Lord, if you want me to be a minister, I am going to be the best one that I can be." I realize now that that may have been a self-centered prayer, but I remember telling a friend about my prayer. He replied, "Wilmer, you're going to be a great preacher, and God is going to use you far beyond Pennsylvania."

The wider church community, many of whom I didn't even know, sent me letters saying, "See this as God calling you to ministry and get more training." Even though my parents didn't finish grade eight, they supported and encouraged me to get additional training, which I did. Janet and I attended Ontario Mennonite Bible Institute in Kitchener, Ontario for three winters after we were married. After this, I became the pastor of the Mennonite Church in Tavistock, Ontario.

Milo Shantz, a businessman and entrepreneur, became a friend soon after we moved to Ontario. "Maybe I should go full time into business," I once said to Milo. He responded, "Wilmer, you wouldn't be satisfied. Business would not be enough for you." In 1990 Milo called and asked me to consider becoming the president and CEO for Habitat for Humanity Canada. Initially I said, "No." When he called the second time, I said, "No." When he called the third time, I was working on a sermon and I remembered the story of Samuel and Eli. I looked up at the ceiling and said, "God, is this you calling?"

As I reflected on my career and my ministry, a value my parents taught me was that when you sense God calling you, say "Yes." I could say yes to being ordained at age 18 because of what my family and church taught me. Part of my baptismal vow was that if God called me to be a minister, I would say yes. My parents also taught me to accept the support of the faith community. In every major decision in life, my faith community listened to my struggle and provided support so that I could take risks and move forward even when the path was not very clear.

It was January 21, 2000 at a Habitat for Humanity Canada national board meeting that the board of directors and I came to irreconcilable differences. Some directors thought that it was time for a change. Millard Fuller, Habitat for Humanity International founder, told me that I was so focused on growing the Habitat program across Canada and Jamaica that I didn't spend enough time talking with the board. I had gone to that board meeting unaware that there was a problem. Later that day, I tendered my resignation. I chose to resign because I did not want to hinder the building of more Habitat homes across Canada and Jamaica, a program that I loved and still love today.

Emotionally, for me, it was like going forward at 120 miles an hour and hitting a block wall. I felt like a failure. I couldn't say goodbye to my staff at the national office or the Habitat affiliates and supporters across Canada or staff and supporters in Jamaica. Even though I still don't fully understand what happened that day, I understand that I should have spent more time on board issues. I am grateful that my family and my community of faith stood with me during those traumatic days. God used them to protect me from myself and to protect my leadership gifts for the future.

With their support and encouragement, I was now able to put full-time energy into TourMagination which had not had a full-time president in its 30-year history. A line I often used when people across Canada and Jamaica were disappointed that they didn't get money to build a Habitat home or when things didn't work out right was, "When one door closes, God opens a window." When the door closed on my leadership at Habitat for Humanity, I chose to give full time to implement TourMagination's mission statement of "building bridges among Mennonites, other Christians and faiths around the world through custom-designed travel."

I believe my prayer in the washroom as the airplane was approaching Vancouver in November 1999 remained in my spirit and protected me from bitterness and protected my leadership gifts for continued use in God's kingdom.

SECTION

LIVING
OUR
FAITH

DON'T LEAVE
JESUS BEHIND

Mennonite churches across Tanzania in Africa all have a bell in the tower to call people together for worship. Seeing the bells in those church towers brought back memories. Hearing the ringing of the bell on the Musoma Mennonite Church during a visit in 2007 was a sacred moment.

When I was ten years old, a missionary visiting our farm said to my parents, "The bell on your washhouse is needed to call people to Jesus in Africa." The bell was no longer being used to call people to dinner on our farm since everyone had watches. So my parents had the bell taken down, crated, sent to Baltimore and put on a ship to go to Africa. We were informed that Clyde Shenk used the bell on a meetinghouse.

I heard that bell being used to call people to Christ in Tanzania. After I brought greetings to the Musoma Mennonite Church, the current minister said, "Please go back home and tell your family that the bell your parents gave to call people to Christ is still being used to this day."

Visiting that church in Tanzania was a moving experience for me. Beside me in the pew sat Joe Shenk, since deceased, whose father, missionary Clyde Shenk, had built the meetinghouse in the 1950s and received my parents' bell. The building was packed the Sunday I visited. Every bench and all the aisles were full of people. Joe said to me, "My father built too small a meetinghouse."

The theme of the service was, "Don't leave Jesus behind." When the Apostles' Creed was spoken, no books were used. Even the small children recited the creed by memory:

> *"I believe in God, the Father almighty,*
> > *creator of heaven and earth.*
> *I believe in Jesus Christ, God's only son, our Lord,*
> > *who was conceived by the Holy Spirit,*
> > > *born of the Virgin Mary,*
> > > *suffered under Pontius Pilate,*
> > > *was crucified, died, and was buried;*
> > *he descended to the dead.*
> > *On the third day he rose again;*
> > *he ascended into heaven,*
> > *he is seated at the right hand of the Father,*
> > > *and he will come again to judge the living*
> > > *and the dead.*
> *I believe in the Holy Spirit,*
> > *the holy catholic church,*
> > *the communion of saints,*
> > *the forgiveness of sins,*
> > *the resurrection of the body*
> > *and the life everlasting."*

As we traveled in various regions of Tanzania and Kenya, we found that Jesus Christ is very much alive in African culture. A hotel receptionist was not hesitant to ask me if I believe in Jesus Christ. Initially, I was taken aback by the question. In a church, one of the choirs sang about taking God's word to the people. They sang, "Do you have the word of God to share? Don't leave Jesus behind." They went on, "Your love and your actions will show for the world that you love Jesus."

An African fable tells about a man who found Jesus. He regularly shared his testimony. Every time the community gathered for worship, you could count on him being one of the first to share what Jesus had done in his life.

But then he got busy. He wrote out his testimony and told his wife to fold the paper and put it in a safe place where he could always get it to share.

Several years later, friends visiting his home asked, "Do you have a testimony to share?" The man asked his wife to please go and get his testimony so he could tell the visitors what God had done for him. Some time later his wife came back. "Where's my testimony?" asked the man. His wife replied, "I have very sad news. I found the box where I put your testimony, but your testimony is gone. A rat has eaten it."

The bell ringing on the Musoma Mennonite Church serves as a symbol for me. Initially, its ringing brought tingling to my spine because of the faithfulness of my parents in responding to the need in Africa. Its ringing reminds me that following Jesus transcends culture, time and generations. Each generation develops its testimony of what it means to believe in Jesus Christ and how that belief impacts our lives. The fable tells us that it is important not to lose that testimony.

THE PEACE OF CHRIST

Mohammad Yunus from Bangladesh was the 2006 Nobel Peace Prize winner. While visiting the Peace Prize Center in Oslo, Norway, our tour group observed his statement: "Poverty is created by systems we created; we can fix the systems, we can cure poverty."

Often during a worship service, the worship leader or minister will say to the congregation, "Please share with each other the peace of Christ." It is an invitation to turn to a neighbor and shake hands or embrace one another and say, "May the peace of Christ be with you."

During my years as chair of the Leadership Commission of the Mennonite Conference of Eastern Canada, I enjoyed working with congregations who were searching for a minister, evaluating their congregation, or were in conflict over pastoral leadership. When we gathered, I encouraged them to sing the hymn, "Heart with loving heart united," written by Nicholaus von Zinzendorf and to think about the words they were singing:

Heart with loving heart united, met to know God's holy will.
Let his love in us ignited more and more are spirits fill.
He the head, we are his members, we reflect the light he is.
He the master, we disciples, he is ours and we are his.

May we also love each other and all selfish claims deny,
so that each one for the other will not hesitate to die.
Even so our Lord had loved us, for our lives he gave his life.
Still he grieves and still he suffers, for our selfishness and strife.

Since, O Lord, you have demanded that our lives your love
should show,
so we wait to be commanded forth into your world to go.
Kindle in us love's compassion so that everyone may see
In our fellowship the promise of a new humanity.

(From *Hymnal: A Worship Book,* Brethren Press, Elgin, Illinois; Faith and
Life Press, Newton, Kansas; Mennonite Publishing House, Scottdale,
Pennsylvania, 1992*)*

In February 2007, after visiting Kenya, Tanzania and
Zimbabwe, our tour group was in Johannesburg, South Africa where we dispersed to different flights to North America.
I was the only one of our group on a 747-400 aircraft bound
for Toronto when it was discovered that my seat was broken.
The plane was almost filled when a flight attendant came to
my seat and said, "Mr. Martin, you have to get your luggage
and come off the aircraft; your seat cannot be fixed." The
plane was oversold by thirty passengers; there were no spare
seats.

I looked at him and said that I would get off the aircraft only if he promised to get me on a plane operated by
one of the five other airline companies that were departing for
North America in the next two hours. He said he would try. I

disembarked with him and we rushed to the other carriers. He worked hard, but all the flights were oversold.

Two hours later we were standing by the curb, waiting for the hotel bus to take me to a hotel. He looked at me and asked, "Mr. Martin, what do you do?" I responded, "Why do you ask?" He said, "When I came onto the plane and saw you standing there, I was prepared to get a lot of vulgar words from you. I have worked with many people of your status but I have never met a more gracious person. What do you do?"

I looked at him and became "weepy" inside because I was frustrated and did not feel gracious. I wanted to go home to my family, not spend the night in Johannesburg. But I told him TourMagination's mission statement of "building bridges among Mennonites and other Christians and faiths around the world through custom-designed travel." He thanked me for my graciousness and kindness to him and said that he too was raised Christian.

I have learned that we share the peace of Christ more by the way we act than by the words we speak. In order to build bridges of understanding, we must first work together. It is only after listening to one another that we can move to the deeper level of being able to discuss issues of faith. Jesus said, "Peace I leave with you, my peace I give to you…do not let your hearts be troubled and do not let them be afraid" (John 14:27).

The King Is Among Us

When King Hussein of Jordan died, his son Abdullah II was sworn in as King of Jordan. The new king wanted to learn about his kingdom. He decided to dress as a commoner so the people of Jordan would not recognize him. He moved throughout the kingdom to learn what was taking place.

King Abdullah learned that people were not treating each other with respect and were not being honest. As word spread throughout Jordan that the new king was dressing as a commoner to observe what was taking place in his kingdom, things began to change. Border guards began to treat people with respect. People began being kinder, for they did not know when the person they were serving might be King Abdullah.

James 3:17 says, "Wisdom from above is first pure, then peaceable, gentle, willing to yield, full of mercy and good fruit without a trace of partiality or hypocrisy, and a harvest of righteousness is sown in peace for those who make peace."

More than thirty years ago, while I was pastor at the Tavistock Mennonite Church in Ontario, I took a Canadian

Association of Pastoral Education course at London Psychiatric Hospital. In one of the courses, I was instructed to plan my funeral service: hymns to be sung, scriptures to be read and to write my eulogy. The impact of that assignment on my life was profound. It impregnated my mind with the thought that some day, at my funeral, people would reflect on my life. I am a citizen of God's kingdom. Therefore, I try to remember that the way I live has an impact on the community locally and the world in which I move, which transcends national boundaries.

What hymn or eulogy will reflect my life? is a question worthy of careful thought. One hymn that I requested to be sung at my funeral was written by Nicholaus von Zinzendorf in 1742.

"The Lord is king, O praise his name,
o'er all the earth his grace proclaim!
From age to age, from day to day,
his wonders grow more gloriously.

O see the mighty hand of God,
his love and mercy changeth not!
His blood and righteousness avail,
his grace and pardon never fail!

This shall the song forever be
of saints before the crystal sea:
O Christ, that on the cross hath bled,
hath safely through life's valley led.

O Star that lights the pilgrim's way!
Our Lord of lords, our hope and stay!
The head to whom we homage bring,
the rock to which our faith may cling!"

(From *Hymnal: A Worship Book,* Brethren Press, Elgin, Illinois; Faith and Life Press, Newton, Kansas; Mennonite Publishing House, Scottdale, Pennsylvania, 1992*)*

While visiting the Isle of Patmos in Greece where John the Revelator had a vision which is recorded in the Book of Revelation, our guide asked us to look at the image on an icon. As we stood looking at the icon, she reminded us that one will not find a shadow on an icon while looking at it. The icon is a perfect revelation.

There is a lesson for all of us in the image of an icon not having a shadow. Do our lives show clearly that we have chosen to be citizens of the Kingdom of God?

I WANT TO BE A CHRISTIAN TOO

arina is a young Paraguayan who lives at a boarding school for deaf students operated by Helga from the Chaco. Helga told us that one day Carina said to her, "Where are your parents?" Helga answered, "They died." "But really, where are they now?" Carina persisted. Helga told her that their bodies were in the ground, but they went to heaven to be with God. "How do you know if you can't even talk to God?" asked Carina. "When I pray, I talk to God," responded Helga. "I know that God has prepared a place for me in heaven and I will go to be with God when I die because I love God and God loves me." Carina said, "I can't go there. My grandfather would never let me go."

Another student said, "Carina, when Helga goes to heaven, she won't need crutches anymore. God will give her a new leg." Helga, who is now in her 60s, had polio and one leg was amputated when she was 14 years old.

Helga said that Carina was quiet for three days. Then she came and said, "I want to go to heaven too." Carina, who is deaf, had a very bad temper; she would kick and bite and throw things. Helga told her, "When you love God and want to go to heaven, you must be kind and not do these things and then when you get to heaven you will be able to talk and hear and dance." Carina wanted to be a dancer. "Since that day," said Helga, "there has been a drastic change in Carina's behavior. It has been a difference like night and day."

God receives his children with the open arms of parental love. The apostle Paul said in Romans 1:19-20: "For what can be known about God is plain to them, because God has shown it to them. Ever since the creation of the world, his nature, namely his eternal power, has been clearly perceived in things that God has made." God has revealed himself in the created universe. When we visit Iguazu Falls in Brazil, one of God's wonders, I enjoy listening to the comments of tour members: "Isn't it wonderful what God has made?" or "I've always wanted to see this."

In Asunción, Paraguay, a number of Mennonite businesses hire chaplains to work among their employees. They hold a one-hour Bible study weekly during business hours. The employees get paid to come to the Bible study. If an employee or a member of his family is in the hospital, a chaplain will make a pastoral visit. The businessmen provide family counseling, classes on parenting and childcare and they buy clothes for the employees' children as well as their school books.

The Funk family operates an air conditioning business there which is thirteen years old and has one hundred and fifty employees. I heard one of their woman employees say, "I was away from God and didn't love God anymore. But since coming to work for the Funk family, I have given my life to God who lives in my heart. I find that I have more time for my family and I am happier."

Anebal, our coach driver, was listening to the conversation. He said, "They are building moral character within their employees."

Anebal and I had many conversations. He learned that Janet and I had celebrated our 40th wedding anniversary several years ago. This was amazing to him. He said, "It's very unusual in Paraguay, since Paraguayan men want younger women." So I used this opportunity to interpret to Anebal Janet's and my commitment to God to be faithful to each other. I told him that Janet and I are not perfect; we've had to ask each other for forgiveness and we try to put into practice the teaching of Jesus Christ which we call the Golden Rule: treat the other person the way that you would wish to be treated. Since we love God and Jesus Christ, God's spirit gives us the ability to maintain commitment and faithfulness.

May God give us the courage to integrate our faith into our daily lives. There will be times when we sin against God and we will be convicted but, as the scriptures remind us, God's grace is sufficient to forgive us.

RESPECT FOR
AUTHORITY

A group of young adults on a service tour in Jamaica with me visited Dunn's River Falls in Ocho Rios. With the two Jamaicans hired to guide our group of thirty, they started to walk up the falls. One guide said, "All those who want to take the easy route stay to the left; those who want to take the harder route follow me to the right." Most of the young people followed the guide to the right. He then chose a young woman to go first. I watched as Allison made her way through the falls. At one point, the group actually had to walk under the falls and they couldn't hear or see or smell anything; they could only touch. Allison obviously was capable and she was soon standing at the top, coaching the others who tried to follow her example and the directions of the Jamaican guide.

It was a beautiful scene. At one point there was quite a wait as one of the group said, "I can't do it, I can't see, I can't hear." Allison yelled, "Yes, you can! Take one more step!" And she did. As soon as she touched Allison's outstretched hand, the young woman had confidence and immediately went to the top. It was a wonderful example of courage in community and respect for authority.

In my early years of ministry at the Tavistock Mennonite Church, a course in pastoral education at London Psychiatric Hospital had a profound impact on my life. During that course, I came to realize that I am a citizen of God's kingdom first, which through faith transcends my nationality. I am more than a citizen of the United States or Canada. Respecting the authority of God in my life allows me to encounter the community and those around me.

God has called his children to understand that all of us have been given authority. We have to own that authority in providing leadership and we must respect the authority of others. James 3 says, "Show by your good life that your works are done with gentleness, born of wisdom.... Wisdom from above is first pure then peaceable, gentle, willing to yield, full of mercy and good fruits, without a trace of partiality or hypocrisy. And a harvest of righteousness is sown in peace for those who make peace" (James 3:13b, 17, 18).

In the Mennonite church where I grew up and was baptized, the Bible was central to daily living. My parents read the Bible every day at the breakfast table because our family's life centered around the scriptures, the church and our work on the farm. The church had what we called a *Discipline*, a small book that was read twice a year at the time of communion. It taught respect for authority. Our bishop, minister and deacon were called to uphold the *Discipline,* which was designed to assist the church family in understanding the rules and boundaries of living a Christian life in the Washington-Franklin Mennonite Conference of Pennsylvania.

As a young minister in that conference, I felt the weight on my shoulders of interpreting the scriptures and keeping the church family living inside the boundaries of the *Discipline.*

After God called me to attend the Ontario Mennonite Bible Institute, my ministerial credentials were transferred to the Western Ontario Mennonite Conference. It was during my early years as pastor of the Tavistock Mennonite Church that I realized that God had called me to teach the scriptures and to call people to follow Jesus Christ. The judging of faith is between God and the believer.

This understanding was a freeing experience for me as a minister at age twenty-five. It gave me the opportunity to walk with the church family, teaching the scriptures, encouraging the faithful and allowing God to do the rest.

UNTO THE HILLS

The 500-mile journey from Chambersburg, Pennsylvania to Tavistock, Ontario in 1968 was a big move for Janet and me. I had agreed to become the minister of the Mennonite Church there and to work part time for a homebuilder. How could we be sure that this was God's will for us? We prayed about and discussed this important question.

Several hymns came to our memories. One was "Unto the hills around do I lift up my longing eyes," based on Psalm 121 and written by John Campbell in 1877. The phrase "from God, the Lord, doth come my certain aid, from God, the Lord, who heaven and earth hath made" was particularly meaningful. Another helpful hymn, written by Thomas A. Dorsey in 1932, was "Precious Lord, take my hand, lead me on let me stand."

One of the beautiful aspects of looking to God and being instructed through scripture and hymns is the power of the community of faith. When we settled into Tavistock Mennonite Church, we discovered this faith community of approximately 300 members had all the ingredients that we had relied upon at the Chambersburg Mennonite Church. Whether we faced issues related to the household, health care, work, insurance or car repairs, the community was there to assist us and to help us feel safe and secure in God's love and presence.

We were young, expecting our first child. Almost 40 years later, our children still love and visit Grandpa and Grandma Leis, their adopted Canadian grandparents who became part of our family because of their love and support. Our children say they were fortunate to grow up with three sets of grandparents to come to baptisms, graduations, and special family events.

When we follow our sense of call, peace comes from God and is expressed through the community of faith. We were blessed as we settled into the Tavistock community, and were immediately accepted not only by the Mennonite community but also by the broader Christian community made up of German Lutherans and the United Church of Canada. We felt loved, valued and appreciated.

The psalmist David says, "The Lord is your keeper; the Lord is your shade at your right hand.... The Lord will keep your going out and your coming in from this time on and forever more" (Psalm 121:5, 8). In my work within the church, Habitat for Humanity and TourMagination, I have met lonely people who have not been blessed with a community of faith as I have been.

Life experiences teach us that being a member of God's family, incarnating God's word into our inner being, brings with it the responsibility to be a participant in the community of faith. At my father's funeral, I was impressed by the broad spectrum of the community who came to pay their respect for my dad, people who attended church regularly and those who did not. I became aware of my father's impact on people outside of the community of faith, who described him as a kind, generous man, and I was grateful.

As we lift our eyes to the hills, may we remember that our help comes from the Lord who made heaven and earth but also accept our responsibility to make our community a kinder, healthier place as the spirit of Christ shines through us.

GOD DESERVES OUR PRAISE AND GIVES US PEACE

The Chambersburg Mennonite Church, where my family worshipped, had an annual harvest service on a Thursday morning. It was not the usual time for worship. When I asked my parents why we had to go to church on Saturday, they replied, "It is our harvest service. We need to thank God for the good gifts God gives to us, for the crops growing in our fields."

That year my father had to replant the alfalfa because it didn't rain enough for it to mature, but my parents still took the family to worship on a Saturday afternoon. They taught us that God, the giver of life and all good things, always deserves our praise.

The Bible teaches that God, the Creator, gave life to everything on earth. Genesis records the final act of creation: humankind, "The Lord God formed man from the dust of the ground and breathed into his nostrils the breath of life; and man became a living being" (Genesis 2:7).

God has put a choice before us; we can choose life and good or death and evil.

Former US President Jimmy Carter, with whom I had the privilege of working during my years with Habitat for Humanity, is a wonderful role model for choosing good. He honors and respects all forms of life, especially human life. He has a personal commitment to serve God and to help the people of the world learn to know, respect and work with each other. He has said that he feels he can make a difference. Larry King, who often interviewed the former president on his CNN show, said, "I always feel energized after I have an interview with President Carter."

Larry King interviewed President Carter on the 25th anniversary of the Camp David Peace Accord between Israel and the Palestinians which President Carter had hosted. Larry King asked, "Will there ever be peace in the Middle East?" President Carter said, "I continue to pray for it." Larry King pressed on, "Will it be in your lifetime?" "It is possible. I hope I live long enough," President Carter responded.

The Bible teaches that with God all things are possible. In our service for God we claim this promise. We are not assured that all things are possible immediately, that alfalfa will always flourish, nor that all things are easy. Some things, like peace in Israel, are incredibly difficult. Yet God promises that we as God's creation are never forsaken and that we can do all things through Christ who strengthens us (Philippians 4:11).

On a TourMagination service tour to Paraguay, tour participants worked alongside Habitat for Humanity Paraguay volunteers and a homeowner to build a Habitat home for a needy family. Near the end of the tour, one participant told me that he broke his mother's heart when he left Iowa and joined the US Air Force to fight overseas. "Isn't it ironic," he said with tears in his eyes, "that I spent most of my life running away from my Amish Mennonite heritage and now I can't seem to get enough of it. I live in Pinecraft and drive Amish to their appointments every day in Florida and I came with Mennonites to Paraguay to build a Habitat for Humanity home." That man had found peace.

Jesus said: "Peace I leave with you; my peace I give to you. Let not your heart be troubled, neither let it be afraid" (John 14:27). God offers us strength and peace. It is our choice whether we receive God's peace and pass it on.

UNDERSTANDING GOD'S PURPOSE

B ishop Jackson, a medical doctor, was appointed as bishop for the Musoma District of the Mennonite Church in Tanzania. He felt God calling him to church leadership. However, he could not close his medical practice and leave the people of his region without medical service. So he kept his clinic open and had other people cover for him. That left him with no money to carry out his church duties.

Our tour group was moved by his story. A couple from Ohio felt God calling them to provide support for Bishop Jackson and his family. When they returned home, their congregational care group joined them in supporting Bishop Jackson in his ministry. Bishop Jackson said, "We were blessed by a couple who walked with us when we were in a very dark corner."

The Christian Church is growing very rapidly in Africa. The Tanzania Mennonite Church grew by 12,000 members over a two-year period, but their church lacks business experience. Bishop Jackson said, "Your church in North America is blessed with many business people who bring their leadership ability and their wealth to assist the church program and its growth. This is important ministry. Please keep doing it in serving God."

The government of Tanzania is pushing the Mennonites to establish a liberal arts college at their Bible College. They want them to establish a Mennonite university with three campuses, including one at the Shirati Hospital that would offer a medical degree. The government wants the Mennonites to build this university, calling it the Mennonite University of Tanzania. But the Mennonite leaders are feeling caught and are drawing back. It feels to them like a huge undertaking. Yet they feel called by God and the government and they want the counsel of the rest of the church.

We have all been in places where we experienced such a spiritual moment that we wanted to stay there and glow in it. Once when Jesus took Peter, James and John up a mountain, the disciples saw Moses and Elijah appear and talk to Jesus. As they were leaving, Peter said to Jesus, "Master, it is good for us to be here; let us make three dwellings, one for you, one for Moses and one for Elijah" (Luke 9:33). When we were with the churches in Africa, a number of the tour members referred to this Bible story and said, "Let's just stay here."

Music is one of the evangelism tools of the African churches. The African music moved us and the story of their suffering and how God is blessing their ministry in spite of their suffering and poverty spoke to us in a very spiritual way. In every service we attended, there were youth, adult and women's choirs. They sang and danced and wanted us to rejoice with them that the rate of AIDS is dropping across Africa.

At Menno Kids, a school operated by the Mathari Valley Mennonite Church in one of the poorest areas of Nairobi, the children sang and recited poems for us. Four young children said a poem:

> *AIDS, AIDS, have mercy,*
> *AIDS, AIDS, have mercy.*

AIDS is decreasing throughout Kenya where the infection rated dropped from fifteen to five percent in 2007 due to education, billboards and road signs. We were told that people used to think AIDS was caused by witchcraft but now they know the truth about AIDS and they encourage people to follow the teachings of the Christian church. They say that the Christian teaching of monogamy and faithfulness is the best solution to the spread of AIDS. However, it is still a major problem with more than 200,000 victims living with this disease in Kenya.

I asked Ramon, a school teacher, when I met her at the Musoma Church what the slogan "Stop AIDS, keep the promise" meant. She said that a Christian organization was trying to educate young people in schools as to what causes AIDS. They are calling them to promise to follow the Christian principle of fidelity.

David, the psalmist said, "The Lord is my light and my salvation, whom shall I fear? The Lord is a stronghold of my life, of whom shall I be afraid?" (Psalm 27:1).

Jesus made it clear to his disciples that even though he was going to leave them, they need not have any fear for the comforter, the Holy Spirit, would come upon them and God's Spirit would always be with them. The Tanzania church and we, too, can rest with contentment in that promise.

The Biblical Financing Plan

Movements such as the anti-slavery movement, women's suffrage movement, and civil rights movement have changed the course of human history. Habitat for Humanity is a Christian movement of people who are concerned about their neighbors, who believe it is unacceptable for families to be forced to live in poverty.

Habitat for Humanity is based on the biblical financing plan. In Leviticus we read, "If any of your kin fall into difficulty and become dependent on you, you shall support them; they shall live with you. Do not take interest in advance or otherwise make a profit from them, but fear your God; let them live with you. You shall not lend them your money at interest taken in advance or provide them food for a profit. I am the Lord your God who brought you out of the land of Egypt, to give you the land of Canaan, to be your God" (Leviticus 25:35-38).

Habitat for Humanity believes it is morally and ethically wrong to profit from the poor. Homes are built at no interest and no profit and homeowners must put in sweat equity (volunteer labor) to help build their own homes. Mortgages reflect what it actually costs to build the homes, and when the homeowners pay their mortgages over twenty years, the money goes one hundred percent into building more homes in the community.

From 1991 to 2000, as president and CEO for Habitat for Humanity Canada, I accepted the challenge to build the Habitat program across Canada and in Jamaica as a call from God and God blessed me during that decade of my life. Thousands of volunteers joined the program which grew to include all the provinces of Canada and Iqaluit in the Northwest Territories and across the country of Jamaica.

Building these homes is a sermon of God's love. A businessman in Edmonton who volunteered sent me a kind letter in which he said, "I am so lucky that I can be one of Habitat's disciples in Canada."

When Jesus was asked, "What is the greatest commandment of all?" he answered, "Love the Lord your God with all your heart, and with your soul and with all your mind...and love your neighbor as yourself" (Matthew 22:37). Habitat for Humanity provides an opportunity for people of all walks of life, of every faith and persuasion, to put this teaching into practice.

One of the philosophies of Habitat that intrigues me and many business people is the principle of capital, not charity. Habitat challenges people of compassion to provide the initial capital through gifts and non-interest loans to build or renovate simple, decent homes for the inadequately sheltered. Construction is a cooperative venture between volunteers and the homebuyers.

The Habitat vision generates a lot of energy for it truly integrates the concepts of justice, compassion and kindness. People sometimes ask the volunteers, "Why would you pay your transportation, lodging and meal costs and donate your time to work and sweat to build a house for a family you don't even know?" The answer can come only from the soul of the volunteer.

The biblical financing plan does not embarrass people by saying, "I am a rich person and I am going to give you poor folks something." It is a partnership. At a house dedication, Eleanor spoke to the one hundred and thirty people gathered on her front lawn where just five days before there was nothing except a foundation. She referred to the familiar story of two men walking along a shore where many starfish had been washed up on the sand. Every once in awhile one man bent down, picked up a starfish and threw it back into the water. The other man chided him, "Look at all these starfish that are going to die. Why do you do that?" They walked a little farther and again the man bent down, picked up a starfish and threw it into the water, saying, "That one is not going to die." Then Eleanor, with her voice cracking, said "Thank you for throwing me and my family back in."

Habitat for Humanity believes that we must develop a conviction that the poverty cycle can be broken. It is always encouraging to hear how a family's life has been changed after they have an adequate house in which to live. One father said, "My children and my wife and I don't fight like we used to. My children are eager to go to school and I feel like I am worth something." That is what Habitat is all about: building families, building lives, building hope.

It is amazing how the lives of volunteers are changed as well. Volunteers, touched by the stories and the partnerships with people in need, continue to come back, wanting to help.

To be in partnership with others does indeed change our lives. Habitat and the biblical financing plan are committed to building hope and community among people in need and those who are willing to give of themselves and their dollars to make a difference in the world.

FROM WHERE DO WE RECEIVE OUR STRENGTH?

"If we confess our sins, he is faithful and just to forgive our sins and to cleanse us from all unrighteousness" (I John 1:9). This was the text for my first sermon in 1964. Preaching that sermon was a difficult experience since I was only eighteen years old. Many changes have occurred in my life since that time. As I look back, I am grateful for God's presence with me.

Yoshino Hosoki tells the story of her family in Japan, when people did not have the freedom they have today. Soon after her mother died, her father was arrested because he had spoken critically of the government. Before Yoshino's father went to prison he said to her, "I will take my Bible with me. Every morning at ten o'clock you and I will read the book of Job together. You will be at home, I will be in prison, but we will be doing the same thing at the same time."

That is what Yoshino did. Times were hard since she had to coordinate life at home where there were seven children. Members of their church also provided support. After two months, her father was freed from prison. She talked about how they received strength every morning as they read the Bible, her father in prison and she at home. Yoshino, now a grandmother, says, "God took care of us and we received strength from reading the scriptures together."

In 1981, when the Mennonite Church and the General Conference Mennonite Church asked me to be a member of the Human Sexuality Task Force, I dreaded this assignment but also felt called to serve. I raised the issue with the Board of Elders and the Church Council at Erb Street Mennonite Church where I was pastor at that time. "I may embarrass you," I said. "It is such a sensitive area. What might other people say about your minister serving on a sexuality committee?" One member looked at me and said, "When did we start making decisions of faith based on what other people might say? If you feel called by God to serve, we will stand with you."

As children in Vacation Bible School we sang, "The Lord is in his holy temple; let all the earth keep silence, keep silence before Him." We receive strength as we keep silence before God, surrounded by a faith community. Our faith community encourages us to confess our sins, failures and fears. We can encourage new beginnings since we have encountered God's forgiveness.

We also receive strength when we are faithful in the stewardship of financial resources. Most individuals give out of abundance but some people give sacrificially, when it hurts. Many years ago, a couple who loved music, who were just married, were saving to buy a record player. One evening in a church service the worship leader presented a tremendous need and challenged people to give sacrificially. Later that week, I learned that the young couple had given the money they had saved for their record player to help meet this need. They said, "We will save to buy a record player later."

The scriptures suggest giving a minimum of ten percent of our resources to God's work. Christians usually give first to their faith community, which challenges them to be faithful. My parents sacrificed to send my brothers and me to Lancaster Mennonite School for our final two years of high school. They didn't have the resources, but my mother thought it was important that her sons have a few years at a Mennonite high school. I am very thankful for her vision.

Making sacrifices for our children comes from walking close to God. Christian parents are willing to make sacrifices so their children get proper training, regularly attend church and Sunday school, have opportunities to build good relationships with their peers and their church family, and have opportunities to participate in church-wide events. Do we think about how our choices of church attendance, vacations, the magazines and books we read and the television shows we watch affect our children? On more than one occasion, I heard my mother say to my father, "Omar, what kind of an example is that to our sons?"

John Ruth's three granddaughters and his son, playing a guitar, produced a CD entitled "3 skuzins and a funkle." One hymn they sang was "Sweet hour of prayer." John told me that these three girls sang this hymn to their great-grandpa as his aged father was dying. It wasn't only the 101-year-old man who had moisture in his eyes as they sang. God used those three great-granddaughters to give strength to the old man to maintain his faith as he went to be with God. Think of that hymn and the strength it also provided for those who witnessed it being sung.

GOD PLACED US HERE FOR A PURPOSE

I n January 1997 my wife Janet and I were privileged to be in India for the Mennonite World Conference Assembly. One of the Mennonite communities we visited was Raipur where Janet and I were assigned to stay with a family. We were already overwhelmed with what we had observed: tremendous poverty, people everywhere and a culture that we did not understand.

We lay in bed, hearing strange sounds and smelling strange odors. I said to Janet, "God has us here for a purpose." We prayed for patience, wisdom and understanding. We also remembered Jesus' words to his disciples in Mark 6, "Come away by yourselves to a lonely place, and rest while."

My spirit was deeply touched by the tremendous need in Calcutta. I had never been in a country of nine hundred and fifty-two million people with forty percent of the population living in poverty. Daily we observed people cooking their meals, bathing, and sleeping on the streets. We observed the sisters at Mother Teresa's house joyfully doing their job, busily caring for the children in cramped conditions. The sisters claimed God's presence and rejoiced that they could have a part in turning the darkness of child poverty into an opportunity as they prepared children for adoption.

Living in the Western world with all its comforts and resources, we miss opportunities to experience God's presence in our day-to-day living. Daily I pray for our staff at TourMagination, for our tour leaders and tour members that, as they interact with one another, they may experience the miracle that takes place through friendship, new discoveries and community-building.

God often transforms experiences into holy moments. While I served as president of Habitat for Humanity Canada, volunteers built a house in New Brunswick. Frank McKenna, former Premier of the province, joined us in celebrating the dedication of the "Home for Christmas." Premier McKenna said, "Habitat volunteers are people who put the Christmas spirit into practice twelve months of the year."

During the ceremony, Maria, the mother of the family that was getting the new home, was invited to come forward to receive the key to their new house. As she stood with her husband and children, waiting for the key, she began to sob. When the key was handed to her, her whole body was shaking. Her husband then spoke for the family as Maria held the key. "I want to thank you with a story," he said. "In our village in El Salvador, the priest had a contest with a prize for the individual who could create a piece of art that depicted the present and the future. Everyone wanted to win. When the contest was over, everyone gathered to see the winning entry. The priest unveiled it, a sculpture of a child." The new home owner went on to say, "My wife and I want to thank you for giving our family not only a present, but a future."

The late Mother Teresa, who worked among the poor in India, was asked how she accounts for her great success. She answered simply, "I pray." God has called us to be present in this world. Being present brings the reality that we are here for a purpose. We are called to show our love for God, not just by our words, but by our actions.

SECTION

EMBRACING
THE
WORLD

Cleansing and Thanksgiving

The annual Harvest Service at the Chambersburg Mennonite Church was a special time that broke from the tradition of working. I remember as a young boy going to church with my parents on a Thursday morning for this service and it wasn't at Thanksgiving time. The sole purpose was to gather at our meetinghouse to offer praise and thank God for the harvest, even when the crops were not as bountiful as the year before.

Another service I recall attending with my parents as a young person was Preparatory Service, one week prior to Communion Service. At this service, you were required to go before the bishop, minister and deacon to declare verbally whether your life was right with God and others and that you were prepared to take communion. Cleansing was needed to prepare oneself for worship.

When visiting the Temple of Heaven in China, we were told that even the Emperor came two days early to prepare himself for a celebration there.

Former President Jimmy Carter attends the Maranatha Baptist Church in his home town of Plains, Georgia. Only about thirty families are active members and most of them have assigned tasks. Volunteerism is essential. President Carter enjoys teaching Bible classes and usually several hundred visitors come to listen to him. On the several occasions that it has been my privilege to be there, I have wondered what brings so many visitors from across the US and the world to listen to a former president teach the Bible.

President Carter says in his book, *Sources of Strength*: "Some [visitors] have never attended a religious service before and others are pastors and scholars or well-known authors of religious books. For me, and for many of those in the class, there is a surprising element of interest and even excitement in exploring the scriptures together. Like other Christians, our family needs spiritual fellowship, not special recognition or honors.... As I've taught over the years, the ancient texts come alive when I explore them with a searching heart."

It is interesting to observe how the former president integrates scripture with what is happening around the world. He usually spends the first ten to fifteen minutes talking about world events and issues that the Carter Center is working on in more than seventy-two countries, endeavoring to eradicate poverty and disease and to build peace.

Paul says in Romans 12:3: "I say to everyone among you not to think of yourself more highly than you ought to think, but to think with sober judgment, each according to the measure of faith that God has assigned." Cleansing and thanksgiving require us to look at our attitudes and to listen and hear new insights from God's word and from the community around us.

One time traveling through Turkey with a group, we came upon a fabulous country market with bountiful fruits, vegetables and nuts and we decided to walk through the market. Our guide told us that vendors in this market will never have seen westerners or a tourist bus before, but we would be safe and welcome. And we were. As we walked through the market, the vendors wanted to give us their produce. One of them brought chairs and invited six of us to sit in front of his stall so he could serve us tea. Several tour members turned down the tea, for which we were unable to pay. I encouraged them to accept the cup of tea with gratitude. After drinking tea, having conversation and thanking the vendor, we returned to the coach. As the coach pulled away, a number of tour members said that the hospitality and the warmth they experienced required them to have a different attitude toward the Islamic faith. They said, "In experiencing such grace and generosity, all we could do was to offer thanks to God and ask God to help us to extend the same hospitality and generosity in the future."

Teach me thy truth, O mighty one;
From sin O make me free;
Prepare my life to fill its place
In service, Lord, for thee.

Grant me Thy grace for every task
Until thy face I see,
Then ever new shall be that joy
In service, Lord, for thee.

(From *Hymnal: A Worship Book,* Brethren Press, Elgin, Illinois; Faith and Life Press, Newton, Kansas; Mennonite Publishing House, Scottdale, Pennsylvania, 1992)

WISDOM

While in Jericho, we saw a sycamore tree and recalled the story of Zaccheus, an unlikely member of the kingdom of heaven. Zaccheus, a tax collector, had heard that Jesus was coming to Jericho. Since he was short and the crowd was large, he climbed a sycamore tree because he wanted to see the Lord. Jesus stopped under the tree, looked up and said, "Zaccheus, come down, for I must stay at your house today" (Luke 19:5).

Wisdom is more than knowledge or the ability to accumulate learning. Wisdom relates to inner quality and relationships. The gathered people who saw Jesus talking with the tax collector, known for defrauding people, were shocked when they heard Zaccheus say, "Lord, half of all my possessions I will give to the poor, and if I have defrauded anyone of anything, I will pay them back four times as much." Then Jesus said to the crowd, "Today salvation has come to this house because he too is a son of Abraham. For the Son of Man came to seek out and to save the lost" (Luke 19:9-10).

Father Chacour, from I'billin, Israel, who has written the book *Blood Brothers*, operates a church and school program in this West Bank community. When our tour group went to his village, he explained to us the challenge of sharing Christ in Israel, a country where it is illegal to do evangelism. Father Chacour was shaped first by observing how his parents responded to the aggression of the Israelis when they bulldozed his parents' home and olive trees and captured the land that had been in their family for generations. His parents, as followers of Christ, responded with heavenly justice, grace and forgiveness. And they encouraged their son to study for the priesthood.

After Father Chacour finished seminary, he was placed as a priest in the small community of I'billin. More than twenty years later, he is priest to more than the Christian community. He relates to Muslim and Christian students and to the nearby Jewish community. He reminded us that God is not a Christian; God is God. Our understanding so often limits God by making him a "Christian." Father Chacour encouraged us to not to take sides. "If your being here today and hearing my story means that you can no longer be a friend to your Jewish neighbor in North America, then I cannot be your friend. Don't take sides," he said

Then he shared a humorous story: A rabbi sent his son to the United States to study to become a better Jew. While in the United States, the rabbi's son became a Christian. When the son returned to Israel, the rabbi was very upset and he prayed, "God, what have I done? I sent my son to the United States to become a better Jew and he came back a Christian!" God said to the rabbi, "What are you praying? I sent my Son to Israel, and he came back a Christian."

At times, life can become very dark. It is in those moments that we need to rest with confidence and faith in Jesus Christ. We need to examine our own worth and the meaning of life, our joys and our disappointments. Without meaning, sacrifice can destroy us; with meaning it transforms us. It is love that gives meaning.

Father Chacour helped us remember this truth. Before speaking with our group, he asked, "Why are you here?" There was silence. He asked again, "Why are you here? I am not going to begin my presentation until you tell me why you came."

I will never forget the silence and then slowly people began to explain that they were there to learn by hearing his story and to come to a better understanding of what it means to follow Christ in what is known as the Promised Land.

As followers of Christ, we have a vision of who we are and of the meaning of our lives. With God's help even the darkest moments can be transformed into light and beauty. In those moments, we feel God's presence and peace.

THE WORD IS PEACE

D r. Nakhle Bishara from Nazareth Hospital in Israel is a wonderful Christian brother and a member of the Orthodox Church. When he tells our tour groups Jesus' story of the prodigal son, he does so through the eyes of an Arab Christian and that culture, which brings a deeper meaning to the biblical story for us North Americans.

The prodigal son sounds like a rebellious son. If he hadn't been rebellious, he wouldn't have asked for the inheritance while his father was still alive. By asking for his inheritance before his father died, the son is declaring that he wishes his father were dead. Yet, the father granted his son's request. The son gathered his possessions and his inheritance and went into exile. While he was gone, he attached himself to filth. In fact, he attached himself to the lowest possible level, the filth of swine, even to the point of eating what swine eat. In exile, he lived in miserable conditions. It was not what his father had planned, yet it took the son considerable time to discover that. He was miserable. He began to compare his misery with his father's home. He remembered that even his father's servants were living better than he was. It was only then that this son, whom we know as the prodigal son, became aware of his inner longing to be back in the presence of his father.

He reasoned that he would go back to his father and say, "Father, I have sinned against you and against heaven. Please accept me as one of your servants." He wanted to repent. However, when the father saw him from far away, the father rushed to his son and kissed him. He wouldn't even let the son ask if he could return; he welcomed him back. Peace was possible because the son decided that he wanted to be free from the captivity that he experienced in exile.

Dr. Bishara wants us to understand from the parable how full of love and grace the father was. He said that in the Arab culture, the culture in which Jesus was raised, a man would never run. Rather, he would walk upright with dignity. He would stand and wait for the son to come to him. The father would not stoop to kiss him, but rather the son would kiss the father's feet. In the parable, the father did not follow tradition; he was full of grace and love.

The robe in the story is a symbol of status in the community. The robe is what would have been put on the father when he died. The son even received sandals, which signified that the son was a free man. Servants and slaves went barefoot. Everyone knew from the story that the father was giving back all the rights to his son. He was extending grace.

In the story, the father responded to the older brother by saying, "This, your brother, was lost and is now found, was dead but is now alive." The elder brother wanted human justice and revenge; but the father was full of compassion and love.

The story reminds us that when we eat together, we are reconciled. "Get the fatted calf, and kill it and let us eat and celebrate" (Luke 15:23), the father instructed the servants. Normally for a celebration, a host would kill a goat or sheep, which fed about twenty people. A calf fed eighty to one hundred people. The father called for a banquet and he wanted the whole community to come.

Dr. Bishara, from the ninth generation of a family that has lived in the city of Nazareth, is an Orthodox Christian who has worked as a doctor at the Nazareth Hospital for more than twenty years and he has worked closely with Mennonites. "I have worked with many Christians at the Nazareth Hospital," he said, "and I was touched and blessed by working with Mennonites. I discovered that Mennonites were different. I discovered they were not Christians only on Sunday, but they put into practice Christ's principles in their daily lives."

The city of Nazareth has a population of approximately eighty thousand people made up of Muslims and Christians. Nazareth Elite, the Jewish sector in Upper Nazareth with a population of approximately twenty thousand, does not relate to the citizens of Nazareth. In an incident in Nazareth, a Muslim Nazarene shot a Jewish soldier from Nazareth Elite. At that very moment, a Muslim taxi driver stopped. The Jewish soldier said, "Brother, please help me." The Muslim taxi driver jumped out of his brand new Mercedes with its leather seats and lifted the wounded, bleeding soldier into his taxi. He rushed him to the Nazareth Hospital where immediately three doctors (Jewish, Muslim and Christian) performed surgery on the soldier, saving his life.

Sometime later, Dr. Bishara said, the mayor of Nazareth Elite came to the hospital to say thank you for saving the soldier's life. He said, "I have lived in Nazareth Elite for twenty years and have never thought of coming to the Nazareth Hospital. I was always suspicious of the hospital. There was a big gulf that separated us, but you have removed that gulf. I've come to thank you, as my brother, for saving my soldier's life." Dr. Bishara said that the soldier has stopped by every year to thank him for saving his life.

While our tour group traveled through the Plains of Jericho, we reflected on our faith and life as Christians. Joshua 5:9-12 reminds us how God had removed the disgrace that had come upon the children of Israel and how the Israelites worshipped God. They thanked God that they no longer needed to eat manna that fell from heaven because they were able to eat the produce of the land.

On our pilgrimage in Israel, we also reflected on many of the teachings of Jesus. One of our questions relating to heavenly justice or human justice was "Who is in and who is out?" What about the rebellious prodigal son and what about the elder brother who was looking for justice? God does not regard people from a human point of view. Like the father, God extends grace.

In 1984 at the Mennonite World Conference Assembly in Strasbourg, France, Ron Sider gave a moving speech, challenging Mennonites worldwide to establish a Christian peacemaking team. This team of Christians would go where there was conflict in order to share God's love. That vision, that challenge is making a difference more than two decades later. I was moved as I stood before a mural painted on the wall of the new church built in I'billlin, Israel. The mural depicted Christian peacemakers who were willing to make a difference by standing between forces of evil because of their connection with Jesus Christ.

Hear the words of the father in the prodigal son story: "This brother of yours was dead and has come to life; he was lost and has been found" (Luke 15:32).

Joy in the Midst of Suffering

Mary was a participant on a TourMagination service tour to Paraguay. Several months after she and her husband registered, Mary had a minor stroke. It affected her use of her right arm and she needed to walk with a cane. However, she and her husband still chose to participate in the tour. No one enjoyed or got more meaning out of the tour than Mary. I can still see her painting and staining the doors while talking with the Habitat for Humanity homeowners as together they built the house in Asunción.

As our group was visiting Kilometer 81 Leprosy Hospital, an older woman in one of the units who had suffered from leprosy looked at Mary. She reached out her stumped hand and Mary reached out her hand; they squeezed each other's hands and smiled. The image of that gentle embrace and expression of joy in the midst of suffering touched the spirits of the whole group. No words were expressed, but we all had tears in our eyes and understood the meaning of that embrace.

The Haroun family also experienced joy in serving Jesus Christ even in the midst of suffering. Christiane, my daughter-in-law, is from Beirut, Lebanon. In 2007 Janet and I visited Beirut to be with Christiane and Alan and her family at the time of the death of her mother, Raymonde Haroun. We found the funeral services in Christiane's Maronite Christian tradition very meaningful. There were a number of masses as well as visitations, and people were dressed in black. At one funeral mass, Janet was asked to read Proverbs 31:10-31, the scripture about the worthy wife whose value is far beyond rubies. I was asked to read John 15:12-27 which includes Jesus' command: "Love one another as I have loved you. No one has greater love than this, to lay down one's life for one's friends."

Father Tony, in his sermon, said that Mrs. Haroun was similar to the woman described in the Proverbs text. She was a spiritual woman who had been a widow for some twenty-five years. Her husband died when Christiane was only six years old. Christiane's mother not only took care of her own children during the war, but she also opened her home to two other families for two years. With thirty-two people living in the house, Christiane and her brothers and sisters needed to sleep on the floor so the beds could be used by the guests. Christiane's mother was an example to her extended family until the time of her death, Father Tony said. When he visited her, she continued to challenge him to remember the poor in his ministry.

Lebanon is a beautiful country in the Middle East, considered to be part of the Holy Land. When people visit the Holy Land, they visit sites that we read about in the Bible. They walk where Jesus, the Apostle Paul and other apostles walked. We did not have the opportunity to visit Sidon and Tyre in southern Lebanon, but Christiane and her uncle took us to visit the Cedars of Lebanon, which are mentioned more than one hundred and fifty times in the Bible. We saw cedars dating back more than a thousand years before Jesus Christ.

In Aswan, Egypt our tour group visited a program for working children ranging in age from five to eighteen years.

The program is partially funded by MEDA (Mennonite Economic Development Associates). It includes teaching the children how to read and write and about their rights and safety. We visited some of the work places and talked to the owners and the children. These are some of the things we heard:

- "I discovered that girls have the same rights as boys."
- "My boss no longer hits me for making a mistake."
- A business owner said, "I never learned to read or write; I want my child worker to learn."

In one city of one and a half million people, more than five thousand children work. The program, sponsored by MEDA, relates to five hundred children. Sister Barbara operates a residence for working children with no home. She felt God calling her to direct this program since it would be closed if a director was not found. She has taught the children to pray. A Mennonite Central Committee (MCC) volunteer said that when the sister took over the program, there wasn't enough food. The sister said to the children, "Let's cook the little rice we have." They prayed over the food and began to eat, and the rice did not run out.

Our group was filled with joy at seeing the changes in the lives of the children in the program and the joy of the business owners, one of whom said he was very proud of his young employees. He told us that twenty of his former child employees now are mechanics with their own garages. Young Emad's face beamed as he said his dream is to have his own garage some day. He sleeps in the garage at night, goes home on the weekend and all of his wages help support his family. Christ's love calls us to be a presence, to bring dignity, self respect and life skills to children like these, their families and the business owners.

In Cairo, our group participated in the Coptic Pope's Bible study at the Christian Coptic Cathedral. Three thousand people filled the cathedral that night. As honored guests, we were given reserved seats near the front. We could feel the air of expectancy as people gathered more than one hour prior to the Pope's arrival. When the Pope began to speak, there was a hush over the audience; they wanted to hear his words from God. The Pope spoke on the theme, "As for me and my house, we will serve the Lord." He called on everyone to make room for God in their homes and in their lives.

Coptic Christians are invited to give their questions to the Pope if they would like him to speak on an issue. One letter was from a Coptic Christian man who went to work in Saudi Arabia for three years, away from his wife and daughter. He said, "My wife and my mother-in-law will not accept me back. They won't allow me into my home. What should I do?" The Pope said, "Tell your wife how much you love her. Ask her to forgive you for being away so long. Nurture her, inviting her to welcome you back into the fold. Then you will experience joy in the midst of the suffering of separation."

One Christian tradition in Egypt is to tattoo a small cross on your wrist. Emad, our tour guide for Egypt, showed us his cross. He said, "We do this to remind ourselves that we are followers of Christ. We cannot hide the choice that we have made as God's children."

We all face challenges. There are times when we are thirsty and have a deep inner sense of searching and seeking. In this quest, at times we drink water that does not quench our thirst. Yet our faith reminds us that if we drink deeply of the spiritual resources offered by God, we will experience joy in the midst of human and spiritual suffering.

Drink deeply from the resources God offers; take courage and share His love as opportunities come your way.

WE HAVE BEEN BLESSED

Usually in the last devotional before a tour concludes, I ask, "What do we do with the knowledge we have gained from our experiences while on tour?" Back home, people always say, "Tell me about your tour. What was it like?" We have a choice whether to tell people about the disappointment of a hotel or about the beauty and the people we met in the country we visited.

For a devotional in a tour in Israel, I chose to use the words in John 21 where Jesus asks Peter if he loves him, and then tells him, "Feed my lambs.... Tend my sheep.... Feed my sheep."

In our pilgrimage in Israel, we learned about the rich history, culture and setting where the Bible was written. We were in awe of the ministry of Nazareth Village, a first-century village created to interpret the life and teachings of Jesus. Nazareth Village is only five hundred meters from where Jesus lived as a boy. In Nazareth Village, we took the Parable Walk and heard a number of parables and stories, such as the one about the woman at the well, and we heard how the staff tells the teachings of Jesus through everyday activities. Biblical stories come alive when they are shared in the culture in which Jesus lived and walked with his disciples.

We were told of a young executive who works for Microsoft in Tel Aviv who came with his wife and two colleagues to visit Nazareth Village. On the Parable Walk, he was overcome with curiosity. He said as he left, "I never heard of this Jesus of Nazareth before. I am very curious. I want to come and bring more of my staff and talk with you to learn more about this Jesus of Nazareth of whom you speak."

It is hard for us to imagine an executive with university training, in his forties, living in the country of Israel never having heard of Jesus of Nazareth. As tour members, we were grateful for the opportunity to participate and learn about the ministry of Nazareth Village. When we arrived home, we had the choice of sharing this visit as a highlight with those who asked us to tell them about our tour.

When we recognize in our life's journey that we have been blessed, we are reminded that there is a responsibility that goes with that blessing. Jesus said that if you love me, then you will care for those around you; you will offer support and love. Our prayer at TourMagination is that our tours will encourage people to be a little more informed about the issues facing our world, to be a little more loving and caring because of a deeper understanding and to be open to share some of that knowledge with those who have not had the experience.

Back home, we can ask people to join us in pondering the question of the Zimbabwean pastor whose congregation includes many orphans and AIDS victims: "Why has God placed this tremendous challenge on our church in Zimbabwe and you in North America do not have to face this challenge?" We may not find an answer, but we can challenge people to respond. We can tell how a forty-voice youth choir in a packed church in Siberia at a Thursday evening service inspired us and that the octegenarian minister and labor camp survivor said that what we witnessed was possible only because the women didn't stop being the church when the men were taken from the village. "God has blessed us with young people to take the church into the next generation," he said.

Tremendous energy builds in one's spirit through travel, fellowship and discovery with other tour members and the people one encounters in various cultures around the world. These experiences have opened doors we never realized were possible. As we return home, we remember the fellowship we enjoyed, our new experiences and new friends, and we remember that Jesus said that the most important commandment of all is to love God, your neighbor and yourself.

HOSPITALITY: WELCOMING THE STRANGER

In Halifax, Nova Scotia, by the harbor where cruise ships dock and immigration takes place, a huge sign says, "Welcome to Canada." In that same area is a building called Pier 21. In the early 1900s, many of our people were forced to flee Russia, going west with the German army. Mennonite refugees who were slated by Mennonite Central Committee (MCC) to come to Canada entered at Pier 21.

On our tours to the Maritime provinces in eastern Canada, we visit Pier 21. Often a tour member will tell the story of how an ancestor came into Canada via Pier 21. Some tour members go to the computer room to search for an entry about their ancestors who entered Canada here. It is always a moving experience to listen to their stories, which make the film we see at Pier 21 even more meaningful.

Hospitality is a Christian virtue. James 1:27 says: "Religion that is pure and undefiled before God, the Father, is this: to care for orphans and widows in their distress, and to keep oneself unstained by the world." In Romans 12:13 we read that we should extend hospitality to strangers.

In 2007, I was privileged to co-lead a tour to Tajikistan, a Muslim country, with MEDA (Mennonite Economic Development Associates). In Khujand, we were warmly welcomed by the mayor of the city. We met MEDA staff and visited the fields where fruit-growing and irrigation research was taking place. It is a very exciting story.

During our farewell meal together, the mayor gave us gifts, thanking us for coming to visit them and for caring about Tajikistan. He said, "Please go back to America and Canada and thank [the people] for their partnership with Tajikistan. In our Koran, we are taught that when strangers come into your midst, you welcome them because welcoming the stranger is welcoming God. Your coming to us is a gift from God and we want to send you on your way to your home with God's blessing." It was one of those very spiritual moments when your spine tingles.

Being hospitable and welcoming strangers is a command from God. The word hospitality occurs only a few times in the Bible, but the idea appears as early as Abraham when he entertained angels unawares. The concept of hospitality occurs throughout the scriptures.

Our Mennonite people throughout their migrations, many times as refugees, received hospitality from their Mennonite brothers and sisters in a new part of the world. Their faith guided them in offering the Christian virtue of hospitality to their neighbors as they settled in their new country.

In telling their story to our tour groups, the Mennonites of Paraguay always remind us that God placed them there for a reason. This is demonstrated at Yalve Sanga, where programs were developed in partnership with the Indians of the Chaco. Today a hospital and health care, the Yalve Sanga Bible School for training Indian pastors, the co-operative which provides a market for their crops and distribution of food among their people are examples of hospitality. The Mennonite brothers and sisters made it clear that God placed them in the Chaco for a purpose: to share God's love with the Indians, and to share not only faith, love and food, but also life skills as illustrated by the above.

We have a rich heritage and tradition of extending welcome to strangers. In doing so, we fulfill the law of Christ.

KIND
AND WISE

J ames 3:13 says: "Who is wise and understanding among you? Show by your good life that your works are done with gentleness born of wisdom."

There is a fable brought from Vietnam by missionaries: A little boy walking along a path came to a cage with a tiger inside. The tiger said to the boy, "Little boy, please open the door. I am hungry and I can't get any food inside this cage." The little boy answered, "No, Tiger, if I open the door you will eat me. That's what tigers do with little boys they find in the forest."

The tiger said, "No, no, little boy, I won't eat you. I promise! Please open the door because I am so hungry in this cage." And so the little boy, out of his kindness, opened the door and the tiger jumped at the little boy and said, "Now I am going to eat you!" The little boy said, "No, no, no! You promised you wouldn't eat me!"

"Okay," said the tiger, "let's find three wise creatures and we will ask them if it is the way of the tiger to eat the man." And so they walked along. First they came to a water buffalo. The water buffalo listened to the story of the tiger and the boy.

He thought for a little while and said, "The man works the water buffalo very hard in the fields, and when the water buffalo gets old and he is no longer useful in the fields, the man kills and eats the water buffalo. I say, yes, the way of the tiger is to eat the man." So the tiger jumped at the little boy, but the boy said, "Wait, wait, wait! You said three creatures!" The tiger said, "Okay."

So they walked along and came upon a chicken. The chicken heard the story of the tiger and the little boy and the question "Is the way of the tiger to eat the man?" The chicken answered, "I lay my eggs, the man collects the eggs and feeds me until I get old and am no longer able to lay eggs. Then the man kills me and eats me. I say, the way of the tiger is to eat the man." Again the tiger jumped at the little boy, and again the little boy said, "Wait, wait, wait! You said three creatures." They continued to walk along.

They came to an old man. The old man heard the story and the question, "Is the way of the tiger to eat the man?" The man scratched his head and said, "Walk with me. I don't quite understand the question. Where did you say you were when this happened?" The tiger said, "Over there, at the cage." So they walked over to the cage. The old man said, "Now, I see the cage. Did you say, Tiger, you were inside or outside of the cage?" The tiger said, "Inside the cage, like this!" And he jumped inside the cage. The man said, "Tiger, I see you inside the cage, but I don't understand. Did you say the door was open or closed?" The tiger slammed the door shut and said, "It was like this!" The old man locked the cage. He turned to the little boy and said to him, "Son, today you have learned an important lesson. It is wonderful to be kind, but you also must be wise."

Since 9/11 the spirit of fear has been exploited by officials calling countries to settle problems with warfare. *Mennonite Weekly Review* carried the story of the Salford Mennonite

Church's program to promote kindness and wisdom in their community (October 30, 2006).

John Ruth wrote, "What can one congregation do to promote the gospel of peace?" Salford decided to invite its neighbors, including Muslim friends, to think, discuss, sing and eat together around the expression from the Bible, "Be not afraid," which appears two dozen times in the scriptures.

Among the presenters were two Muslims, one from Harleysville and one from Philadelphia, a public school teacher and a United Church of Christ pastor. Listen to what one of the presenters said: "The answer to fear is simply to follow Christ in love." A woman confessed that her family was too polarized by the war against terror to speak to each other about it. At Salford Mennonite Church she could raise her voice.

The spirit of fear exploited by those calling their country to settle problems by warfare was rebuked by a voice telling us, "Be not afraid, for I am your God and will still give you aid." At the Sunday morning service, Daryl Byler, director of the Mennonite Central Committee office in Washington D.C. told the congregation, "I presented your congregation's peace quilt to a White House staffer. The staff person had left the MCC visitors feeling somewhat hopeless, but at the end of the conversation, the staffer added, 'My wife agrees with all the points you are making and I hear these same arguments every time I go home.'"

On Sunday evening, the auditorium rang with hymns, old and new. Many of the selections called out from the audience underscored the weekend's theme of kindness and wisdom. The offering of $4,200 was dedicated to rebuild a war-damaged town in the beautiful country of Lebanon, ravaged by the war between Israel and Syria. The town selected to receive the funds was the home village of one of the weekend workshop's presenters who is Muslim.

On the following Sunday, participants returned to express thanks with emotion as powerful as anything that had happened on the previous weekend. A young Jewish man from Philadelphia, attending that morning as a visitor, was so impressed that he wondered if he could join the Salford Mennonite Church.

In this unique experience, the spirit of fear was rebuked by the voice of Christ, "Be not afraid." John Ruth said, "We tried to share the sense of peace among ourselves and our neighbors." A reporter from the local newspaper wrote a story about the weekend headlined, "Hope is the key idea."

Wisdom is full of mercy and truth. The book of James says that it is revealed when one feeds the hungry and provides clothes for the naked. It is a characteristic of God Himself. Recently a businessman talked about how important it was that his minister had time to take him out to lunch and to listen to him. Two people eating lunch together is a normal occurrence, but in the act of eating, love and compassion were felt and shared.

Hope grows through kindness and from the knowledge that God can surprise us with possibilities that we never imagined. God's faithfulness to all generations is the foundation of hope that carries us into the future.

The Language of the People

I was raised in a Christian home where faith in God was central. My parents taught me that in order to love God, I must also love our neighbors and that my actions are just as important as my words. I am thankful that my parents not only taught this concept with scriptures like I John 3:18, but they also modeled it by the way they lived and related to our neighbors.

When we profess faith in God and model our lives on the teachings of Jesus Christ, the results are spectacular. I was privileged to be part of the Habitat for Humanity Jimmy Carter Work Project in Vac, Hungary. In five days we built ten homes from concrete slabs to finished yards and fences. Six hundred volunteers from countries that had at one time been at war with one another worked together in tremendous harmony to build homes for the ten families. On Friday afternoon, the houses were dedicated and the families received keys to their homes. In the celebration service, President Carter said, "One and one half hours from here in Bosnia, there are peacekeeping forces at work. Here on this site, during this week, we experienced peace and harmony as citizens from twenty-four countries worked together. This is the best peacekeeping force in the world."

President Jimmy Carter donates at least one week a year to work with volunteers to help build Habitat for Humanity homes around the world. The ministry of Habitat is guided by compassion for neighbors in need, believing that every mother, father and child deserves a warm, safe home in which to live. It gives witness to the gospel of Jesus Christ by working with God's people in need by creating a better environment for them to live and work. It also gives opportunity for those who have been blessed to donate and to work alongside other volunteers and people who need a hand up.

Bo and Emma Johnson were the first Habitat for Humanity partner family. They and their five children lived in a shack in southern Georgia. When it came time for the mortgage to be signed, Millard Fuller, co-founder of Habitat, said "Bo, you're the proud owner of this beautiful home; sign your mortgage." That's when Millard learned that no one had ever taught Bo to read or write and so his mortgage was signed with an "X." Within 20 years the Johnsons had paid off their mortgage and that money was used to build more Habitat homes. Their beautiful home was an empty nest as all of their five children, now adults, are in professions: law, doctor of psychiatry, registered nurse, etc. When I think of those five children returning to see their parents with their children and their friends, I wonder what goes through their minds. If their neighbors had not shown compassion and believed in their parents, life would have been very different for them.

Martin Luther is known as the reformer who translated the Bible into the language of the people. At the age of twenty-two he entered the monastery and two years later was ordained a priest. While Luther lectured at the University of Wittenberg in Germany, he engaged in a severe spiritual struggle as he became keenly aware of the deep gulf between God's demand of righteousness and his own unrighteousness.

This was the time of the great awakening. Printing by moveable type was invented in Mainz, Germany. There was a hunger for literature to read. Luther studied the scriptures and began to interpret them for the people. He tacked up what today is known as "The 95 Theses" on the Wittenberg church door for the people to read.

Martin Luther was being challenged by church authorities in Rome and also by Charles V of the Holy Roman Empire. The pope had issued an edict to excommunicate Luther and he urged the emperor to execute it. However, Charles V summoned Luther to appear before the Diet of Worms, a legislative meeting of the Roman Empire in Worms, Germany, to defend his work or to recant.

Our tour groups have stood and reflected on Luther's life in the park in Worms where the building once stood where Luther testified. His life was spared since he was seized at the instigation of his friend, Frederich of Saxony, and lodged for safety in the Wartburg Castle near Eisenach. On a number of occasions we have toured the Wartburg Castle and have been in the Luther Room where Luther, during his imprisonment, translated the New Testament from Greek into German, the language of the people. With the help of the printing press, the Bible could then be read by average citizens.

Luther was a strong personality who could not be diverted from his purpose by fear or argument. He was reported to have said to the authorities at the Diet of Worm, "Here stand I, I can do no other, so help me God."

Also in Germany, in what used to be East Berlin, stands the Church of the Resurrection. In that church, which experienced tremendous damage and deterioration when it was behind the Berlin Wall, there is a statue of Christ. All that remains of the statue are the head and the body. The arms and legs have deteriorated and fallen away. After the wall that divided East and West Germany came down and the church was reopened, there was considerable discussion about what to do with the statue of Christ. Meetings took place and artists were called together to look at how to rebuild it. One night someone wrote a message under the statue which, translated, says, "Christ has no hands but our hands and no feet but our feet."

We are called to be Christ's hands and feet. We are called to show the love of God not just by words and talk but by actions. This, according to Christ, is the language of the people.

The Power of Presence

L uke's gospel records the time when Jesus came to his hometown of Nazareth and went to the synagogue on the Sabbath as was his custom. In the synagogue he read from the scroll of the prophet Isaiah, "The spirit of the Lord is upon me because he has anointed me to bring good news to the poor, he has sent me to proclaim release to the captive and recovery of sight to the blind, to let the oppressed go free, to proclaim the year of the Lord's favor" (Luke 4:18-19).

After Jesus rolled up the scroll and gave it back to the attendant and sat down, the eyes of all in the synagogue were fixed on him. The text goes on to say, "They were amazed at the gracious words that came from his mouth and they said, 'Is not this Joseph's son?'" (verse 22).

Most individuals fail to recognize the power of their presence within the family and the community in which they live. I came to this awareness when I was 22 years of age. My wife Janet and I were studying at the Ontario Mennonite Bible Institute in Kitchener, Ontario. I forget the course we were taking, but I remember the teacher saying to me, "Wilmer, what do you think? You are obviously the leader in this group. When a question is asked everyone looks to you first." I was shocked by his comment. I was not aware that my presence in that group carried so much weight and authority.

There is a responsibility that comes with leadership. There are times when we try to shake off responsibility. I've heard people say, "I have been there, I have done that, I don't want to lead anymore." But there are times when God calls them back.

My father, the late bishop Omar Martin, was ordained as minister at the Chambersburg Mennonite Church in Pennsylvania in 1953. My parents enjoyed studying the scriptures and teaching Sunday school, Bible school and my father enjoyed preaching God's word. At my father's funeral in 2008, people talked about my dad's leadership during those growing years for this congregation and for that district of the conference. His presence as a farmer and as one of the ministers in the conference was felt beyond his awareness. Our dad loved the church, he loved life and people. He, along with my mother, prayed daily for the church. My parents along with four other couples met regularly for Bible study and prayer in our home. My brothers and I remember those prayer meetings in our living room that went late into the night.

What made my father's presence so felt among the church in the 1950s and 1960s was an awakening and deep appreciation for fresh interpretation of the scriptures. But there was more. It was also, I believe, the prayers of the community surrounding my father as the minister and the encouragement of my mother for my dad to take time from farming to study the Bible. I remember her encouragement for him to attend Minister's School at Eastern Mennonite College. Attending the Billy Graham Crusade in Harrisburg, Pennsylvania was also an encouragement to my father in his call to leadership as a minister.

As a young minister, my father endeavored, with God's help, to put into practice what Jesus said is the greatest commandment of all: "To love the Lord your God with all your heart, soul and mind and to love your neighbor as yourself." He endeavored to pass on to the members of his church that which he heard as the voice of God.

Our response to an experience depends not so much on the event but rather on us as individuals. When people around us look to us for leadership, are we willing to interpret what we sense as the voice of God? Some people within the synagogue in Nazareth sensed that perhaps God was speaking through this young man, Jesus. Others only heard blasphemy and they wanted to stone Jesus; however, he passed safely from their midst.

On our tour to China in 2007, our group visited Esther Snader, an English teacher from Lancaster, Pennsylvania, who was teaching at the university in Anjing. She invited our tour group to come to the university and she arranged for us to speak in the English classes. It was a privilege to sit with the students and answer their questions. Three students, who wanted to practice their English, asked why I would bring a tour group to China. I shared with them TourMagination's mission to build bridges among Mennonites and other Christians and faiths around the world. When we are present with other people and we can see the whites of their eyes, hear each other's stories, eat each other's foods, sit in each other's homes, it leads to a deeper understanding and helps to build bridges of peace.

Later one of the students said, "Do you really believe that?" "Yes," I answered. "I have now traveled in more than seventy countries of the world and everywhere I have sensed love, warmth and acceptance. I have also discovered everyone wants the same thing for themselves and their families - peace, harmony, and a safe, warm place to sleep at the end of the day."

God's love is universal; we as agents on this earth are called to be present in sharing his love with those around us.

THE INFLUENCE OF SPEECH

One of my prayers is, "Lord, protect me against my enthusiasm." I love life, I love working with people, sharing God's love and fulfilling TourMagination's mission statement: "Building bridges among Mennonites, other Christians and faiths around the world through custom-designed travel." Sometimes Wilmer Martin's enthusiasm for life causes me to charge ahead when I need to be listening, waiting to hear God's still small voice. I want to recognize my need for God's spirit to "Set a guard over my mouth, O Lord; keep watch over the door of my lips" (Psalm 141:3).

Our tour group had the same guide as a previous Tour-Magination group for our tour of Westminster Abbey in London, England. Before our tour began, the guide told our group that she has enjoyed TourMagination groups. She said she has studied a bit about Mennonites and has read some of the writings of John Howard Yoder. Then she asked me to remind her of the core Mennonite beliefs. As we talked, she said that since leading tours like ours, she too believes although she has not been active in the church.

There is a tendency in some people to settle in, to know a limited subject fairly well and to be content with that. We call this complacency. Complacency can give temporary comfort, but it doesn't carry persons very well throughout life. If a Christian does not consistently study to stay abreast of change, then one's mind is not kept alert and it begins to show in the way in which we serve and relate to others and to ourselves.

Over the past thirty years, I have taken many groups to Germany to visit the Dachau Concentration Camp. This was the original concentration camp. If you study history, you will find there were hundreds of concentration camps throughout Europe during World War II.

In the 1980s, as our TourMagination group of fifty entered Dachau, a man from Texas stopped me at the main gate, waving both arms and saying, "Don't bring your group in here. This is all a lie. It never happened." He spoke with such conviction that there is no doubt in my mind that he believed what he was saying. Yet, as powerful as his speech was, it did not deter me from taking our group into the Dachau Concentration Camp Museum.

Dachau is a place of extreme darkness. Thousands of victims lost their lives there by being starved to death, shot or killed by disease. Even though a sign on the gates at the concentration camp says, "Work brings freedom," those who entered through those gates found anything but freedom.

In 1945, when Dachau was liberated by the US military, the farmers and villagers who lived as neighbors to the concentration camp were forced by President Eisenhower and his men to visit the camp and see firsthand what took place in their neighborhood. Their visit was filmed and our group saw pictures of the neighbors discovering the concentration camp after it was liberated. They smelled the stench, saw dead bodies and the crematorium where bodies were burned. One might ask, how could they live next door and not know what was taking place?

We are invited to speak for those who have no voice. We are invited to follow Jesus' example; called not to perfection, but to faithfulness.

In 2008, waiting at a departure gate at Frankfurt Airport, I heard the sound of a guitar. I discovered a group of approximately forty young people singing and reading scripture. These young people were returning from Sydney 2008, wearing t-shirts that said Global Youth Summit. They were youth from Barcelona, Spain who had been to Sydney, Australia for the Global Youth Summit sponsored by the Vatican and Pope Benedict. The looks on their faces showed that they were enjoying each other and that they were not ashamed of their faith. They were at home, at peace with themselves, challenged by the power of a movement of youth. They were returning to their communities in Spain, inspired by having heard the word of God through their spiritual leader.

There is a game that young people sometimes play called "Pass it on." The leader whispers a statement to the person standing next to him or her who then whispers the statement to the next person and so on. The last person will repeat the message to the group. The point is to see how accurately the message was sent. Usually there is laughter because the message has been distorted since it wasn't heard correctly or it was changed by the new message bearer.

Often we forget how our speech influences those around us. May the words we speak be words of honesty, integrity and truth. The late Dr. Clarence Jordan wrote in the *Cotton Patch Version*, "Let him who is wise and intelligent among you demonstrate, with true discipline of mind, the fruits of a noble life."

RESILIENCE
OF THE
HUMAN SPIRIT

The late Matthias Martin was an Old Order Mennonite harness maker from Hawkesville, Ontario. Matthias never got to travel the world since his church discouraged such travel. He would have enjoyed visiting Anabaptist sites in Europe on a TourMagination trip so I, along with many others, brought the world to meet and talk with Matthias.

In one conversation, Matthias explained that Old Order Mennonites did not buy insurance. If someone goes to the hospital, he said, the community kicks in to help pay the bill. If a barn burns down, the neighbors rally around, build a new barn, bring hay and share their cattle. This is their insurance. A non-Mennonite visitor then said to Matthias, "I suppose that's the best insurance, the community surrounding its members."

The Mennonite Church is a small church throughout the world and it is amazing how it has spread to more than seventy-five countries. In the book, *Gracious Christianity* by Rodney Sawatzky and Douglas Jacobson, the authors discuss the resilience of the human spirit. They say, "Sin is anything that willfully diminishes what we and the rest of creation are meant to enjoy. Sin is living against the grain of God's universe. Whatever particular form it takes, sin always involves a choice to prefer ourselves over others, over nature and over God."

In my travels with TourMagination I have met many Christians, ordinary people blessed by God, who have learned to recognize the reality of sin, repent, make restitution and accept forgiveness. Accepting forgiveness frees people to a new level of resilience of the human spirit.

In Cusco, Peru, we invited missionaries Ron and Regina Shultz and Don Weaver to speak with our tour group. Missionaries first came to Peru in 1987 and the church is growing very quickly there. One tour group member asked the missionaries, "What attracts people to the church?" They said, "The power of the gospel. The power of the gospel changes lives. For example, alcohol is a tremendous problem and when a person who is struggling with alcoholism finds Christ and is freed from this addiction, it affects not only the family, but the whole community. People notice change and they come to church to experience what is happening. Peruvian Mennonites have a strong vision of reaching their people for Christ."

In Paraguay we invited Carlos Wiens, Health Minister under the Frutos presidency, to speak to our group. He was a missionary's son who became a doctor and a surgeon and served at Kilometer 81 Hospital for eighteen years. Former President Frutos is married to a Mennonite Brethren woman and attends the Mennonite Brethren Church on occasion. When the president asked Carlos Wiens repeatedly over five months to serve in his government, Carlos told him, "I am a missionary, I am a surgeon, I am not a person to be on television and on the frontlines." The president kept asking Carlos to use his gifts to help make Paraguay, which was plagued by corruption, a stronger country. "Then I remembered the story of Jonah, and that maybe this was God calling me to this assignment," said Carlos Wiens, and he said yes. Carlos said he is grateful that the government allowed him to lead the Department of Health as a Christian sharing the love he receives from God. He reminded us that as Christians, if we are deeply rooted in God's love, we cannot help but love others in the same gracious way.

C.F. Yake and Orie Miller were two Mennonite pioneers. C.F worked at the Mennonite Publishing House and Orie was one of the founding members of Mennonite Central Committee. One day C.F. phoned Orie and said, "Come over right away. I need to see you." Orie said, "C.F., I'm very busy right now; I'll stop by and see you this evening." C.F. replied, "Orie, it's important. You have to come right now!" So Orie laid aside his tasks and went to see C.F. When he arrived at his house, C.F. was sitting on the front porch, rocking in his chair.

Orie said, "C.F., what was so important that you needed to see me right now? You're sitting here rocking in your chair." C.F. said, "I am so busy, everybody has given me so much to do, I am overwhelmed. I don't know what to do."

Orie listened and then said, "I can tell you one thing, C.F. Not all the tasks that you are being asked to do are from God because God does not overwhelm his children. The scripture tells us that God will not allow any task or things to come upon us that we cannot bear, with his help."

When our tours visit Oslo, Norway, we are privileged to visit the Nobel Peace Center. Alfred Nobel, the man who donated the money to give out this annual award to people who promote harmony and goodwill around the world, made his money by inventing dynamite. He was sorry that he invented it. During World War I his invention was used by Sweden, his home country, for evil and destruction. He was so frustrated with Sweden that he moved the annual Nobel Peace Prize to Norway, where the Nobel Peace Center stands today. Alfred Nobel reminds the world that God has given us intellects and clear minds to help us use his gifts and resources for good, rather than evil.

We were honored to stand in the room with the names and pictures of Nobel Peace Prize winners from around the world, including Desmond Tutu, Mother Teresa and President Jimmy Carter. All have endeavored to follow their convictions, their calls from God to promote peace and harmony and make the world a better place. Proverbs 15:3 says: "The eyes of the Lord are in every place, keeping watch on the evil and the good."

A young man applied for a job as a Morse code operator. After filling out the job application, he sat with seven other applicants in the waiting room. After a few moments, the man stood up, strode across the room to the door of the inner office and walked in. Within a few minutes, the employer escorted the young man out of the office and said to the other applicants, "Gentlemen, thank you very much for coming, but the job has just been filled." The other applicants began grumbling and one spoke up, "Wait a minute! I don't understand. The last one to come in got the job and we never got a chance to be interviewed. That's not fair."

The employer said, "I'm sorry, but in the last several minutes, while you were sitting here, the telegraph has been sending out the following message in Morse code: 'If you understand this message, come right in.' None of you heard or understood it. This young man did and the job is his."

We are often distracted, unable to hear the small voice of God as he speaks in creation, in the scripture and in the life and work of Jesus Christ through the church. May God give us clear minds and calm spirits so that we may follow in the way of peace.

SECTION

INSPIRED
BY THE
WORLD

A PLACE FOR GOVERNMENT AUTHORITY

On our tours to Australia, we visit Canberra, the capital city. We enjoy visiting their House of Parliament and walking through this modern capital building. We are allowed to walk on the roof, which is grass, and look across the beautiful city. Canberra was constructed in 1913 after Walter Burley Griffin, an American architect, won an international competition for the design of the city. The people of Australia did not want the capital in Sydney or in Melbourne, the two major cities. They decided to design a city that Australians would be proud to have as their capital. It was not completed until 1927, when the first federal parliament was convened there.

In every country in which I travel, I meet leaders who want to talk with me, a Christian, about their faith. In 2007 in Tajikistan, a Muslim country, a gentleman came to me and said, "I am a believer also," and he wanted to talk with me about some issues of faith.

Among faith issues for me is the separation of church and state, one of the founding principles of Anabaptism. We are citizens of God's kingdom first. One confession of faith of the Mennonite Church is the "Schleitheim Confession of Faith." Michael Sattler was one of the leaders of the group that gathered in Schleitheim, Switzerland in the early days of our church and produced this document. Sattler was captured by the authorities carrying this simple document that addressed the separation of church and state, the role of leaders, baptism on confession of faith, communion, not carrying the sword, etc. All seven articles highlight the principle that we are citizens of God's kingdom first.

Today we hear a lot of criticism about our world leaders. One would wonder why leaders feel called by God to provide leadership. I have always admired Bob Rae, the former Ontario premier, even though many people feel that he failed in that position. In a conversation with Bob Rae when he was running to become the leader of the Liberal Party and possibly the prime minister of Canada, I asked him why he felt called to lead the Liberal Party. He talked about his inner sense of call to serve his country in this way. Secondly, his wife and people close to him had told him to either stop talking about this inner sense of call or begin to do something about it. Leaders, whether in the church or government or business, need to have an inner sense of call to lead and be affirmed by their community.

There are times on our tours when tour members become intense in their conversations about leaders of government. On a number of occasions I have told tour members what my bishop would regularly remind the congregation when I was a young boy: Pray for those in government who provide leadership. God has placed them in this role for a purpose. The Apostle Paul in Romans 13:1 said: "Let every person be subject to the governing authorities; for there is no authority except from God, and those authorities that exist have been instituted by God."

I thank God for the privilege of having lived and worked in the United States and Canada and for having passports for both countries. I am grateful for the stable governments in both my host countries. As a Christian, I have a responsibility to pray for and encourage those who are called to serve in government, but my faith reminds me that I am a citizen of God's kingdom first.

LEARNING IN JAMAICA

The island of Jamaica is portrayed by the tourist industry of the world as the place to go to enjoy beautiful beaches and all-inclusive resorts. Jamaica's motto, "Out of many, one people," reminds us of the blending of culture and traditions. The main nationalities of origin in Jamaica are African, European, Indian, Chinese, Lebanese and Jewish. The different skin colors of the Jamaican people are beautiful to observe. The world has come to Jamaica and brought along different cultures, traditions and challenges.

In the 1990s, Habitat for Humanity Canada adopted the country of Jamaica as a partner country. They used the tithes (ten percent of the cost) from building homes in Canada to build homes in Jamaica. As president and CEO for the charity in Canada, I was assigned to assist in setting up Habitat for Humanity in Jamaica. Traveling across the island, meeting people who were interested in assisting the development of this national charity, I learned about "day-for-day." This concept, deeply rooted in Jamaican culture, means that you give me a day, I give you a day. This old tradition of mutual support is still very much alive in rural Jamaica and to a lesser extent in urban Jamaica.

It was my privilege in May 2008 to take the Grade 12 class from Shalom Christian Academy, Chambersburg, Pennsylvania, to Jamaica for nine days. This was their intercultural experience, a requirement for graduation from Shalom. Of the 32 participants, the majority saw this as a wonderful opportunity to learn the culture, to serve and share God's love and to interact with Jamaican people. A few were there because it was a graduation requirement.

During the nine days, my goal and commitment was to introduce them to the Jamaican people and the country I have learned to love. Jamaica has had a matriarchal society; historically women provided stability and leadership in the country. Men were brought to Jamaica as part of the slave trade. They were taught to work hard on the plantations, breed and add more children to Jamaica, but they were not taught or trained to be compassionate or family-oriented. This was left to the women, an influence that still affects the country of Jamaica.

I enjoyed watching the students interact with the Jamaicans. We painted at schools and churches. I can still see in my mind the picture of Stephanie teaching a young boy how to hold a paint brush and paint the wall. She did it with such compassion. What a beautiful picture of caringly teaching life skills to the next generation.

As we were painting the school in Claremount, St. Anne's, Jamaica, Mrs. Brown said, "Please don't leave me out." I stopped and talked with her as she showed me a section of her classroom that needed to be painted. She beamed as the students finished painting her classroom. We were able to partner with her because I took time to listen to her.

Audley has been our bus driver in Jamaica for more than 30 years. His story is very meaningful. When Milo Shantz from St. Jacobs, Ontario was raising and selling turkeys in Jamaica, he needed transportation. He found this young man from Retreat in St. Mary's Parish whom he hired to be his driver. Out of that relationship, Milo put his confidence in Audley and took a risk by buying him a bus to drive and to use twelve months of the year. Audley's nickname today is Milo. If you try to find "Audley" at Montego Bay Airport, people look at you blankly, but when you ask, "Have you seen Milo?" they say, "Yes, he's over there."

Audley tells me that Milo took a chance on him and because of that, Audley today owns three buses. He has paid Milo back with interest and has chosen to use Milo's name as his nickname. When I first met Audley in the 1980s, he told me that he was an atheist; today he's a believer and he continues to live out in Jamaica what Milo taught him: take a chance on people, walk with them, believe in them, help them to succeed, and share Christ's love through daily work.

The Apostle Peter reminds us that we are a part of the body of Christ and the way in which we live our lives and receive God's love in the midst of daily routines helps shape who we are. Peter's words to the young Christian church scattered throughout the Roman world come to mind. These Christians had experienced trials, afflictions and suffering. Peter reminded his readers that they were connected to Jesus Christ: "Come to him, a living stone, though rejected by mortals yet chosen and precious in God's sight and like living stones, let yourselves be built into a spiritual house, to be a holy priest to offer spiritual sacrifices acceptable to God through Jesus Christ." (I Peter 2:4-5).

Jamaica has taught me to take time to listen to people like Mrs. Brown and Audley. I heard Audley say, "Walk slowly, listen to the people around you. Milo believed in me; I want to pass this on to others."

LESSONS FROM THE PENGUINS

On our tour of Antarctica in January 2008, we marveled at God's greatness in creating this magnificent part of the world. We were blessed with excellent weather and sunshine that glistened on floating icebergs. We had many sightings of whales and seals, but the most talked about aspect of God's creation was the penguins.

Many people have asked if we saw the Emperor Penguins, the species featured in the film, "The March of the Penguins." These penguins live further south, closer to the South Pole, but we saw many thousands of penguins, primarily Gentoo and Chinstrap penguins. Our naturalist on board the ship pointed out several other breeds.

The penguin is a flightless, aquatic bird of the Southern Hemisphere. Most penguins have a white breast and a black back and head. Many species exhibit red, yellow or orange patches on the head and neck. As their legs are placed far back on their bodies, they assume an upright posture. Their flipper-like wings are short and mostly black.

The penguins' flippers bear little resemblance to the wings of most birds. They usually walk or hop or toboggan along on their breasts, pushing with wings and feet. However, they swim with great speed and agility. Their flippers are their sole means of propulsion. The feet are trailed behind or used in steering.

As our group observed the penguins in the rookery, we learned some life lessons related to humankind. We remembered Jesus' words in Matthew 7:7-12: "Ask, and it will be given you; search, and you will find; knock, and the door will be opened for you. For everyone who asks receives, and everyone who searches finds, and for everyone who knocks, the door will be opened. Is there anyone among you who, if your child asks for bread, will give a stone? Or if the child asks for a fish, will give a snake? If you then, who are evil, know how to give good gifts to your children, how much more will your Father in heaven give good things to those who ask him? In everything do unto others as you would have them do to you; for this is the law and the prophets."

1. We learned from the penguins that when you have trouble, you slide, but you do not change your direction; you move toward your goal. Penguins lay their eggs and hatch their young in a rookery, often many miles from the ocean. We watched the penguins move over the hard rock formations on the path that their ancestors used for generations to approach the rookery. They did not take the easy way.

2. Parents work together. It is amazing how the penguins mate in one of the world's most inhospitable regions during one of the coldest periods of the year, laying and incubating their eggs at temperatures as low as minus eighty degrees Fahrenheit. In general, both

sexes incubate the eggs and feed the young. We saw the Gentoo Penguins changing places, sitting on their eggs or on their young. Normally the males fast during the incubation period. After the egg is laid, the female returns to the sea to feed and bathe, while the male sits on the egg and fasts, sometimes for up to six weeks, defending the nesting area and incubating the egg. When the female takes over the incubation, the male goes to the sea to feed and he returns in an amazingly short time. Both parents share the responsibility for feeding the young penguins by regurgitating fish. The chicks feed on the rich food from their parents' beaks and the young penguins grow very quickly.

3. Penguins are not distracted by their surroundings, but are focused on raising the next generation. Most penguins do not have a nest; they choose a territory among the rocks. They find boulders, sticks and other debris to form a safe place to lay their eggs and hatch their young. We did, however, see Gentoo Penguins use small pebbles to build a nest. It was interesting watching how the Gentoo Penguins tried to steal stones from neighboring nests. It was like they were playing a game and every once in awhile one would slip away with a stone. Even though a neighbor stole a stone, the penguin was not distracted from its primary task of caring for its young. It stayed on the nest.

Our naturalist, in the teaching session, told us not to take sides when we are out on our excursions. There are natural enemies of the penguin, including the Leopard Seal, the Killer Whale and in the case of young chicks and eggs, the Skuas. He said, "You will observe that the weak are eaten by the Skuas." At Half Moon Island, I saw a huge Skua flying with a live penguin hanging from its beak. The Skua flew away from the penguins to a place alone on the snow to eat the captured bird. It was hard not to take sides, to think of the parents who had just lost their young; and yet this is part of the life cycle. I looked back across the rookery and saw that even though tragedy had struck, thousands of penguins were not distracted from their mission of being a community and caring for their young. They continued to maintain their stromg community of penguins.

We recalled Jesus' words: "Look at the birds of the air; they neither sow nor reap nor gather into barns, and yet your heavenly Father feeds them. Are you not of more value than they?" (Matthew 6:26). It was a fabulous experience to observe thousands of penguins nesting and feeding their young, and the Skuas in their role of helping to keep the rookery healthy and free of disease. One tour member observed - and all agreed, "God's creation in the cold Antarctic is magnificent." We were in awe and also gave thanks for safety in our travels.

YOU CANNOT HIDE WHAT MOTIVATES YOU

D id you ever stop to think that you hear everything you say? Every thought or word, every frustrating or angry utterance, every tender word of love that has ever come out of your mouth has been heard by your ears and registered in your brain. David in Psalm 141 says, "Keep watch over the door of my lips.... But my eyes are turned toward you, O God, my Lord; in you I seek refuge; do not leave me defenseless" (verses 3 and 8).

One of the joys and privileges of leading a tour group is the opportunity for conversation with people who are on a vacation with the chance to gain new insights from other places in the world. Traveling together for two weeks lets me begin to learn the thought patterns of tour participants and their understanding of what it means to follow Christ.

The Apostle Paul wrote to young Timothy that he should study to show himself approved unto God, a workman that needs not be ashamed, rightly dividing the word of truth. Our minds and talents are gifts from God. What we do with those God-given endowments is up to each of us as individuals.

In Coventry, England, our tour group visited and worshipped at Coventry Cathedral which has been rebuilt next to the ruins of the original cathedral. The Germans bombed the city during World War II because Coventry was an industrial city that produced a lot of armaments and had a huge railroad station. Usually cathedrals were used as landmarks in bombing raids and were not bombed since they were houses of God. This was not the case in Coventry. Part of the burned out, destroyed cathedral stands as a monument of destruction and darkness.

Coventry Cathedral today is an active place of worship which reveals the commitment of the Coventry community to restoring their place of worship after the bombing. When we were at the morning worship service, the cathedral was filled with more than one thousand worshippers. We were there on the Sunday of the ordination of deacons and priests for the Coventry diocese. We witnessed and heard approximately fifteen people take their vows to proclaim the message of Jesus Christ and be faithful to God's word and to the teachings of the church.

One of the songs written by John Lennon and sung by The Beatles is entitled "Strawberry Fields." Strawberry Fields is an area in Liverpool where John Lennon ran and played as a boy with children from a nearby orphanage. Before Lennon was assassinated, one of the charities he supported was this orphanage. His widow and his estate continue to fund children at the orphanage to this day.

You cannot hide what motivates you. John Lennon's music made him rich and famous, but he remembered poor orphans like those with whom he played as a boy. The people of Coventry Cathedral built a new cathedral next to the ruins of their former cathedral as a symbol that God's light is stronger than darkness. A wonderful sculpture of two people embracing stands among the ruins of the old cathedral. The sculpture reminds us that in the face of destructive forces human dignity and love triumph over disaster and bring people together in respect and peace.

TRUST
AND TEAMWORK

One of the ghettos in Kingston, Jamaica, called Majesty Gardens, is located within walking distance of the free zone where cotton is brought in on ships from the United States. People from the ghetto make garments from the cotton which are then loaded back onto the ships and returned to the United States. The garments say "Made in the USA" because the free zone is controlled by the US.

One would think that the workers from Majesty Gardens would have a decent place in which to live, but Majesty Gardens in reality does not live up to its name. Thousands of people live there without running water or sewage facilities. People survive with one water hydrant and plastic bags to dispose of their waste.

A businessman who came to the ghetto every Sunday afternoon to teach Sunday school befriended a third-generation ghetto boy. The businessman, who had no children of his own, became attached to Patrick. He encouraged him and helped him get to school and then go to community college. Patrick continued to live in the ghetto.

In 1993, Habitat for Humanity began building homes in partnership with the people of Majesty Gardens. The businessman introduced me to Patrick and suggested that I ask him to work for the Majesty Gardens Habitat for Humanity program. I asked Patrick how we could choose the families to receive Habitat homes since every family was in need of a decent place to live. Patrick said that was no problem. He said that we would build ten homes and after they are ready and dedicated, the first ten families to move in will be those who have put in the most hours of sweat equity in building the homes and have paid the largest deposits. That was the only Habitat for Humanity project in which I have been involved where we did not have one complaint about our choice of homeowners. Everyone knew the guidelines and they all rejoiced with the first ten families to receive their homes.

Words from Ecclesiastes 4 remind us of teamwork and trust. "Two are better than one, because they have a good reward for their toil. For if they fall, one will lift up the other; but woe to one who is alone and falls and does not have another to help. Again, if two lie together, they keep warm; but how can one keep warm alone? And though one might prevail against another, two will withstand one. A threefold cord is not quickly broken" (verses 9-12).

One of the challenges we face in life is the willingness to trust people in leadership and to become team players. The first time I walked through Majesty Gardens, I walked with a government official who wanted to give us the land and a church worker who had gained the trust of the residents. I was uncomfortable because of the comments I heard from some of the residents. There was an amazing difference when I began to put my faith and trust in Patrick. As we worked beside him, building more than forty homes under his leadership, it became clear that I could walk anywhere in the ghetto and feel safe and welcomed.

One day we came to the work site and discovered that some of the steel used as rebar to form the walls was missing. Word spread that someone had stolen rebar from Habitat for Humanity. Soon a resident brought back the steel with an apology and I knew that we didn't need to fear that things would be stolen again from the Habitat for Humanity project at Majesty Gardens.

On a more recent trip to Kingston, Jamaica, I visited Majesty Gardens and was amazed to see how the initial leadership of Patrick and Habitat for Humanity is spreading throughout the ghetto. The welcome sign at the entrance to Majesty Gardens is the same, but what I saw inside was very different. The first Habitat for Humanity homes are still standing and many of them have been expanded. Other building is also taking place. The people who still live in shacks seem to be improving their conditions with the meager resources they have. This is not to say that crime, corruption and misuse of power are not still happening in this community, but I was reminded of the Apostle Paul's words: "We do not live to ourselves, and we do not die to ourselves. If we live, we live to the Lord, and if we die, we die to the Lord; so then, whether we live or whether we die, we are the Lord's. For to this end Christ died and lived again, so that he might be Lord of both the dead and the living" (Romans 14: 7-9).

I was grateful that we went beyond our comfort zone and chose to begin building Habitat for Humanity homes in Majesty Gardens and that God gave us Patrick so that we could gain trust and create teamwork within the ghetto. Patrick had interpreted the program so well to his fellow residents that they applied for homes and made deposits.

We had made the decision to begin to build homes in Majesty Gardens but had not yet broken ground when we gathered for a question and answer period on the Habitat for Humanity program. I will never forget one dear lady who raised her hand and asked, "Is there no one in the world poorer than we are? You told us that we are getting these homes because the money used to buy building materials comes from Canada. Canadians, when they build a home in Canada, are tithing ten per cent to help build a home in Jamaica. Is this correct?" I said yes. She went on, "We want to help someone, too. Can we not give ten per cent of the money that we put into these homes to help someone in another country?"

It was one of those moments when your spine tingles and you get goose bumps because you recognize a very powerful and spiritual moment. Generosity is at the core of every human spirit but it takes teamwork and trust for it to be developed and expressed. We do not live to ourselves; we do not die to ourselves. Let us live, following the example of our Lord.

WATER:
A GIFT FROM GOD

ater is a very important resource, a gift from God. The psalmist David said, "He leads me beside still waters" (Psalm 23:2).

On our journey in Egypt, we visited many sites, learned about the pharaohs and saw antiquities from more than four thousand years ago. We also had discussions with Mennonite Central Committee (MCC) workers, leaders of the Coptic Church, business owners and children who worked and are supported through the Mennonite Economic Development Associates (MEDA) program.

Egypt, a country of seventy-two million people with twenty-two million living and working in Cairo, is known for its desert climate. The Nile River is a main source of life for Egypt, providing water for bathing, drinking, irrigation, and navigation. Water determines the vitality, strength and vigor of animals and human beings. It is essential to health and general well being. Tour members who do not drink enough water when it is hot tell me they do not feel well. After drinking a bottle or two of water, they regain their vigor and strength.

A physical body needs water. The scripture points out that the human soul needs the water of the spirit of the eternal God. Jesus said in Matthew 5:6: "Blessed are those who hunger and thirst after righteousness, for they shall be filled."

Our group attended the Coptic Cathedral in Cairo for the Coptic Pope's Bible study. We were given reserved seats near the front as honored guests among the three thousand people who filled the cathedral that night. We could feel the air of anticipation among the crowd which gathered more than one hour prior to the Pope's arrival. When the Pope began to speak, there was a hush over the audience. They were thirsty to drink in his word from God.

George, an Egyptian, has worked for MCC in Cairo for eighteen years. He told us he was working for MCC when he met his wife. When he took her to meet the MCC country director, he was not sure how she would accept his working in a Christian program. As they were sitting and talking, another MCC couple dropped in. The couple smelled like kerosene. The couple explained that when they came home they found a statue standing in front of their house. It hadn't been there in the morning when they left. As they stood looking at it, the eyelids fluttered. Then they realized it was a man who had been rolled in hot tar and then set in front of their house. The tar had hardened and he could not speak or move except to flutter his eyelids.

The MCC couple quickly went to a nearby gas station, got kerosene and began to work on his body, wiping away the tar until all was removed. They took him to a car wash and hosed him down with a high speed pressure hose; then they took him to their home and poured ointment on his body and gave him clothes from their closet. They did not know his name. To this day, MCCers do not know who this man was or who tarred him.

George said, "My wife-to-be was overcome by the love of God that this couple showed to this stranger. They saved his life."

We live in a world where there is much chaos and confusion, religious indifference, suspicion and hatred. I have been encouraged by the bridges that are being built in Egypt through programs sponsored by Mennonites through MCC and MEDA.

May we, as God's children, drink deeply from the spiritual resources God offers, and may we have the courage to share his love as opportunities come our way.

DOORS CLOSED, DOORS OPENED

I da Habermehl lived her life for others. As her pastor, I was privileged to hear her story and to sit with her as she faced death in 1989. She still loved life and would have preferred to be given more time. However, her testimony was clear: "I am ready to go to be with God if this is his will."

A message that I have given to many people as a pastor, as a president and CEO, and to my children is, "When a door is closed, look for the one that God is opening for you." Ida had learned to be content, to be satisfied and to watch for the door that God opened. She did not finish grade eight because her peers at school made fun of her speech impediment, but through medical science in Philadelphia her speech was corrected and she was able to go on to Toronto Bible College and graduate in 1947. Initially, she wanted to go back to Philadelphia to thank the city for assisting in her healing; however, US immigration said no.

In 1952, her friend Dorothy convinced Ida that she was needed for God's work in Chicago. When US immigration allowed Ida to go to Chicago and the door was opened by the invitation of her friend Dorothy, Ida said yes. She moved to Chicago and serving the needy in the form of social work became her life's work. Ida's sisters told me that she gave so much of herself to others.

William Mann Phelps said, "During my lifetime, I have known great sorrows and at times felt the black of depression. I live everyday as if it were the first day I had ever seen and the last day I would ever see." When Ida went to the hospital for an operation, she talked with me prior to her surgery and shared with me and her nieces and nephews that she wanted to die the way she lived. "When they operate on me, if they find they cannot do anything to save my life, don't put me on life supports. I lived my life for others in service in Chicago. I don't want resources wasted on keeping my body alive."

Her wish was put on her chart, but on the day following her surgery she was on life supports. Her nieces and nephews asked me what they should do. We talked to the nurses and doctors and reminded them of Ida's request. Ida being on life support was not opening a door. It was closing a door, wasting the gifts of the medical team and the financial resources that could be used for others. When this was explained to the doctors and nurses, there were tears. The medical team said that they enjoyed serving this unusual woman whose belief in life after death was encouraging. Her life was a short 71 years; however, she saw those days as a privilege to share the love that God had bestowed upon her.

We have a choice to look at life with pessimism or optimism. A retired businessman once told me that he felt certain that God was calling him to be a pastor in Pennsylvania. In fact, when his name was put in the lot, he had a dream as to which book he should choose. He was certain that in the book would be the slip of paper saying the lot had fallen on him.

On the day of the ordination service, when it was his turn to choose a book, he took the one he saw in his dream. He was certain that when the officiating bishop opened the book it would be revealed that God was calling him to be the pastor of this congregation. He was not called that day and he was never called to be the pastor of a congregation. His call was to be the president and CEO of a family corporation in the food industry. He said he was disappointed and confused on the day of ordination. He felt the door was closed by the system, while in his dream he saw the door being opened. Thirty years later, he realizes that he has had many opportunities to minister in God's name in the corporate world and he is forever grateful that he was obedient to God's call.

In the Paraguayan Chaco, the Mennonites, working alongside the Indians, helped built a colony on thousands of hectares of land for the indigenous people. They also built a school and a hospital. During our visit, a nurse from the United States took our group through the Yalve Sanga Hospital. After she explained the program, I said to her, "I appreciate your enthusiasm as you interpret the program. You must enjoy your work very much." She responded, "When one is called, then it is a joy to serve."

Another story from Paraguay comes from John and Clara Schmidt who were sent as missionaries to open a leprosy hospital eighty-one kilometers east of Asunción. The hospital was to be a thank you to the people of Paraguay for providing a home for the Mennonite immigrants who had to flee Russia. Neighbors did not appreciate that the country gave this tract of land to the Mennonites to build a hospital to care for lepers. They did not want that hospital in their backyard.

One day when John was out on house calls, six men came to the hospital grounds to destroy the construction that had begun. Clara saw their crowbars and tools of destruction. She saw doors closing. She told her staff to heat water and she invited the men in for tea. She provided hospitality. The men sat quietly as they drank tea and had refreshments while Clara shared the vision of what they hoped to do for the citizens of Paraguay. The men left without causing any destruction.

Millard Fuller once visited the Federal Prison Institution in Texas where young people with life sentences are incarcerated due to crimes against citizens of the United States. Habitat for Humanity invited the federal prison to partner with the poor. Prisoners built doorjambs, walls, headers and other products from lumber brought into the federal institution for use at the Habitat site. In this way, the prisoners experienced windows of opportunity when doors were closed around them. The warden wanted the founder of Habitat for Humanity to come and speak with the prisoners. Little Johnny, a boy whom Millard guessed to be ten or eleven, walked up to him, held out his hand and said, "I want to thank you for coming and talking to us nobodies. We know that you are a very busy and important man, but we want you to know that we appreciate that you came to talk to us."

Johnny spoke with such conviction that Millard said, "I couldn't help but weep. I told Johnny that he is making a huge difference in the lives of a Habitat family and because of his efforts another family has the opportunity to be freed from poverty."

Longfellow once wrote "Footprints in the sands of time, footprints that perhaps another might take again, footprints that give hope."

Communication
Through
Imagination

Often when I receive letters from clients they misspell the name TourMagination; they write Tourimagination. They have captured what TourMagination wants people to think: that we travel with imagination. They often ask, "Where did you get the name TourMagination?" TourMagination began in 1970 with two Mennonite church leaders and friends, Jan Gleysteen and Arnold Cressman, who worked at the Mennonite Publishing House in Scottdale, Pennsylvania.

Both men were attracted to H.S. Bender's work on the Anabaptist vision. This was a time of awakening interest in our Anabaptist heritage and rediscovering our Mennonite roots in western Europe. Arnold and Jan decided to plan a tour. Arnold had the skill to plan tour details. Jan, who was born and raised in the Netherlands and had ridden his bicycle all over western Europe after World War II, knew the locations. So in 1970, they took a group to Europe, the first TourMagination tour, and amidst those conversations the name TourMagination was born.

Imagination is described as "the process of forming a mental image of objects or perception or thought in the absence of the concrete or external stimulation."

Some people cannot understand why anyone would be willing to travel to places where no buildings are left. I have seen people looking among growing crops who find a piece of tile or an old foundation of a building constructed generations ago begin to cry. This happened in the Ukraine with an 83-year-old man who so much wanted to go back there. When our TourMagination group got to one farm, he and I walked through the field and found a few remains of the foundation of a Mennonite Brethren meetinghouse. He held a piece of tile and sat there and cried. His imagination brought the memory back and he said, "My father helped to build this meetinghouse." We cried together, remembering the struggle of God's people in that place. "The eyes of the Lord are in every place, keeping watch on the evil and the good" (Proverbs 15:3).

Hans Christian Anderson was a Danish author and poet most famous for his fairy tales which have been translated into more than one hundred and fifty languages. Millions of copies continue to be published all over the world. A museum in Odensee, Denmark, where he was born, displays his life and history. What do fairy tales have to do with our society, and why are they so popular?

Hans Christian Anderson was raised in a poor family. He displayed great intelligence and imagination as a young boy. His parents, particularly his superstitious mother, didn't quite know what to do with this young boy who sat at home making clothes for his puppets and reading all the plays he could lay his hands on. Throughout his childhood he had a passion for memorizing plays and reciting them using his wooden dolls as actors. Shortly before his death he wrote, "Most of the people who walk after me will be children, so the music at my funeral should be upbeat, and keep the music in little steps so the children can be comfortable." One of Anderson's critics asked if he would write his autobiography. He claimed it had already been written in his famous fairy tale, "The Ugly Duckling." As I read his fairy tales, I am impressed with the moral and spiritual values that Anderson shared by telling stories using animals, birds and mythological characters to communicate messages of hope and peace.

It is a challenge for humankind to think outside of the status quo. What we experience in the present seems so real and strong. We are comfortable and wonder sometimes why we need to consider changing. One of the issues that requires our imagination today is our environment and particularly our resources.

TourMagination is partnering with Mennonite Economic Development Associates (MEDA) and Mennonite World Conference (MWC) to promote MEDA's new carbon offset energy fund. Carbon offsets for travel is not a new idea; having a Mennonite option is. Now we can offer a way for TourMagination clients to participate in this bridge while showing their concern for God's creation. More information can be found at TourMagination's website at www.tourmagination.com.

As we use our imaginations, may we do so by honoring the principles of our faith.

ONE MIND

I n China, our tour group visited beautiful Tiananmen
Square which shows China's pride. One could not help
but be impressed by the friendliness and orderliness of
the crowds, estimated at one million people, visiting the square
that day. A sign read: "Millions of people, one mind." This sign
reflects one of the reasons for the orderliness of the people in
China. They have a common focus created by a strong, central
government; an ideology and structure which creates in them a
willingness to follow with one mind.

When our group was getting off the bus at the Three
Gorges Dam, I asked the driver to open the back door, but he
did not respond. I then asked our local guide to please open the
back door so that our people could get off the bus faster. She said,
"It is against policy." She smiled and walked away. The Chinese
government provides stability for its people. This is illustrated
by a strong foundation and the orderliness of the Communist
government, which they claim is communism and democracy.

The late Erie Sauder was a man of deep faith with a giving spirit. In 1976 he founded the Sauder Farm and Craft Vil-

lage in Archbold, Ohio, an eighty-acre, non-profit, living history museum, created to preserve the lifestyle of the pioneers who settled the swamp area of northwest Ohio. On occasion our tour groups visit the museum and we are always impressed with his vision. Sauder Furniture is known for the production of church, office and home furniture that is pre-cut and assembled in your home.

Sauder was also one of the founders of Mennonite Economic Development Associates (MEDA). Business people volunteer their time and resources to assist others in making a living. Erie Sauder traveled to Paraguay to assist refugees from the Soviet Union and Germany to develop the wastelands of the Chaco and to turn what they called the "Green Hell" into profitable, habitable land. Touring the museum, one discovers that Sauder was a man with a strong faith in God. He never forgot that everything he had was a gift from God to be used faithfully.

In Deuteronomy 4:1-2, Moses commanded Israel to obey and follow God's laws. As they remembered God's promise to them and obeyed God's laws, they gained an honorable reputation in the eyes of other nations. Each time they heard God's laws, they made a choice, and each time that they became doers of the law, they took a step forward in their relationship with God.

On one occasion, Milo Shantz traveled with our tour group to Paraguay. He was one of the young businessmen who had worked with Erie Sauder to begin the MEDA program. Milo shared with the group how Erie, a businessman about 30 years older, impressed upon him the need to see life as a gift from God. In response to what we have received from God, we share with others.

These values provide a strong foundation and create one mind and purpose. The path of obedience to God is simple and provides direction in life. Each day we face many choices which become markers that record our past and give direction for the future.

John Newton was a sea captain of a ship that carried slaves from Africa to be sold to other countries. He traveled to the Ivory Coast of Africa many times. Newton had turned his back on his family and his values; however, his friendship with John Wesley and the Quakers helped him to see his moral depravity and he became an advocate and a strong preacher against the slave trade.

On December 31, 1772, John Newton was remembering his life as a slave trader. He sat with his wife Mary, who had a profound impact on his life, and thought about what it meant to follow Jesus Christ. He knew that he needed to preach. The next day, on January 1, he read the scripture, "One thing I do know, that though I was blind, now I see" (John 9: 25). Hours later he sat by his fireplace and wrote the lines, "Amazing grace! how sweet the sound, that saved a wretch like me! I once was lost, but now am found, was blind, but now I see."

Nearly 250 years ago, John Newton was used by God to remind Christians around the world of a common focus and a challenge to follow Jesus Christ and accept God's grace, mercy and forgiveness.

Boulet serves as a step-on guide for our tours in Turkey, a country with sixty-five million people, ninety-nine percent of whom are Muslim and one percent Christian. Turkey is a democracy; it is not a religious government. Church and state are separate. Only approximately thirty percent of the people who are practicing Muslims go to the mosque regularly. However, Turkey has a high view of the family. One does not see beggars on the streets; families look after and help one another. They would not think of having older people go to a seniors or nursing home to live. Boulet paints a very ideological picture for our group when he shares the story of his people. He says, "If you saw a person who didn't have a place to stay or food to eat begging in the street, you would take him home."

At the end of one of our tours, Boulet asked me if it would be all right to bring his wife and daughter to meet our group, to spend the day with us in Istanbul and on the boat ride on the Bosporus Sea. He told me that he had never introduced his wife to a tour group in his nineteen years in this role. His daughter sang the Turkish national anthem and some other songs for us, as well as an English ABC song that she had learned. Then he wanted us to sing for his wife and daughter since he enjoyed our singing. So we sang the US and Canadian national anthems and the hymn, "Praise God from whom all blessings flow." We told him that this was our Christian anthem. As we sang, the three of them looked at each other. Finally, we sang, "God be with you till we meet again."

Parents are called to be an example to their children, but how can they be an example if they do not have the time and opportunity to be around them or if children don't hear conversations between adults and listen to their stories? Boulet's ten-year-old daughter made us all smile as we observed that her father was calmer and different when his wife and daughter were with him. Children do that to us adults. We cannot help but be touched when a child squeals with delight or grabs your hand to show you something. It makes you feel warm inside.

Erie Sauder and John Newton's lives serve as examples long after their deaths. Thank God for their lives because they remind us that life is a gift from God. As we accept God's grace and live our lives according to his principles, we make the world a more grace-filled place.

WALLS
THAT DIVIDE

W hen walking on the Great Wall of China, it is hard
to fathom that this wall extends over fifteen hundred miles. The wall is built of earth and stone
with many places faced with brick in the eastern parts. It is
fifteen to thirty feet thick at the base with an average height of
twenty feet. The wall has watchtowers that rise as high as forty
feet. It is hard to comprehend that this fortification along the
northern and northwestern frontiers of China was built before
Christ. Its construction was begun in 228 BCE and finished
in approximately 204 BCE. The wall was built as a defense
against barbarian hordes.

We know of other walls that were built to divide and
keep people apart. The Iron Curtain was a barrier to communi-
cation and free exchange of ideas between countries. We recall
the scene on television when President Ronald Reagan stood in
Berlin and said, "Tear this wall down." Many of us watched in
awe as the wall came down several years later.

As a Christian community, we are committed to remove barriers that divide. In the synagogue in Nazareth, Je-

sus said, "The Spirit of the Lord is upon me, because he has anointed me to bring good news to the poor. He has sent me to proclaim release to the captives and recovery of sight to the blind, to let the oppressed go free, to proclaim the year of the Lord's favor" (Luke 4:18-19).

Walls that divide today are oppression and poverty. Sub-Saharan Africa is the only place in the world which yields less food year after year. Today, farmers in the region are forced to contend with challenges about which their parents never dreamed. As the population grows, they have no choice but to cultivate their land more intensively. With fewer nutrients to feed the plants, the yields are lower each year.

Starvation used to be a threat for many parts of the developing world, but starting in the 1940s an effort to improve crop yield known as the Green Revolution swept through much of Asia and Latin America. It gave small farmers a measure of security for the first time. In 1970, Norman Borlaug, a Rockefeller Foundation scientist and pioneer of this effort, was awarded the Nobel Peace Prize for his work on the Green Revolution. Through the efforts of the Green Revolution, the amount of food in the developing world has doubled since 1980.

On September 12, 2006, the Rockefeller Foundation and the Bill and Melinda Gates Foundation launched a new partnership to help Africa start its own Green Revolution. The Gates recognize that if the West continues to get richer and Africa continues to get poorer, the walls that divide become more pronounced. I was impressed with the partnership outlined on the Bill and Melinda Gates Foundation website, "New Hope for African Farmers." They said that the goal is to develop one hundred new crop varieties that are adapted to the local conditions in Africa within five years; to train African breeders and agricultural scientists who can spearhead this process in the future; to guarantee reliable ways to get high quality, locally adapted seeds into the hands of small farmers through seed companies, public organizations, community organizations; and to network ten thousand small merchants largely responsible for providing supplies and knowledge to African farmers.

Why are people like the Gates and earlier those behind the Rockefeller and Ford Foundations concerned about the poor of Africa? Each of these organizations is based on Christian traditions and values. They may use different words, but underlying their purpose is the teaching of Jesus. They have a vision of a new Africa where farmers are not threatened with hunger and poverty, where children are not facing starvation, where people can look toward the future with promise.

As Christians, our challenge is to look at walls that divide and work to assist in removing them. Those walls may not be as noticeable as the Great Wall of China, the Berlin Wall or the wall dividing Israel and Palestine. Let us offer thanks for the generosity of the foundations mentioned and let us, too, look for ways that we can remove walls, release captives, provide sight to the blind and freedom to those who experience oppression.

THE AUTHOR

Wilmer Martin served as a Mennonite minister for twenty-eight years in three congregations in Pennsylvania and Ontario. During this time, he served on many conference boards in southwestern Ontario and on church-wide boards for the Mennonite Church in North America. He served as co-chair of the task force that produced the book *Human Sexuality in the Christian Life* (Herald Press). He was President and CEO of Habitat for Humanity Canada from 1991 to 2000 and was instrumental in building a national program across Canada and organizing and developing a national program in Jamaica.

In 2000 Wilmer became the first full-time president of TourMagination, dedicating his ministry to expand the TourMagination program. He has traveled to more than

70 countries to build bridges among Mennonites and other Christians and faiths. His love for pastoral ministry, encouraging persons to learn to know one another and building peace are his passions.

Wilmer was born and grew up in Chambersburg, Pennsylvania. His post-secondary education includes graduating from the Ontario Mennonite Bible Institute, Kitchener, Ontario, earning a B.A. degree from the University of Waterloo and a Masters in Theological Studies from Waterloo Lutheran Seminary. He and his wife Janet live in Waterloo, Ontario and are members of the St. Agatha Mennonite Church.